"*In Grace for Your Waist*, Janelle takes you into her soul's "closet." She authentically wore for most of her life that led to her f are in your healing process, her practical application of God's promises will encourage you to get on the path to freedom."
Nancy Stafford, Actress (TV's "Matlock"), Speaker, and Author of
Beauty by the Book: Seeing Yourself as God Sees You

"I am so encouraged by Janelle's honesty and authenticity in *Grace for Your Waist*. The path toward healing is a long, painful one and one you shouldn't go alone. In the pages of this book, Janelle meets you where you're at and brings words of health and healing through her own experiences and, most of all, through God's truths."
Susan Merrill, Founder of iMOM.com

"I have known Janelle for years and applaud this remarkable book, penned from her heart. An accomplished story-teller, Janelle candidly shares her journey of inner healing that motivated sustained weight loss. Her style is witty yet wise, compelling yet convicting, personal yet practical. Readers will value the action steps that conclude each chapter, inviting them to move incrementally toward their own future story of God's grace. Throughout, Janelle focuses attention where due: shameless God promotion and honor to the One she loves and serves."
Quinn Schipper, Founder and CEO of OIKOS Ministries
Author, *The Language of Forgiveness*

"Several years ago, I had the privilege of meeting Janelle as she shared her story, how she is becoming who God made her to be. Watching her journey continue to unfold is pure joy. Janelle, thank you for inviting us on the journey with you, and for encouraging and empowering us to become who God made us to be!"
Emily Cummins, Founder of BecomingMe.TV

"You can hear Janelle's heart in every word of this book. She gives generously from her experience and healing from a very personal place. My favorite quote from this book is: 'Very often we want our situation to change, when God desires to change us with our situation.' I also loved the action steps and prayers at the end of each chapter. The action steps make it doable. This book is destined to help many with a common problem we all face. Janelle's story is not only inspiring, it's empowering!"
Carla Bridges, Manager at Ruth's Christian Bookstore and Women's Ministry Leader, Countryside Baptist Church, Stillwater, OK

"Size has nothing to do with the relationship with Christ. If it did, it would be inversely proportional in the case of my dear friend Janelle Khanyasile Keith (Khanyasile in Siswati means light). As she shed the pounds, she grew in such massive and profound faith, it is astonishing. We are blessed by her Godly wisdom and courageous spirit. Her real-life story is the real deal, a journey to her identity found and anchored in Christ."
Mitch Hildebrant, Pastor, Hills View E Free, Piedmont, SD

"In *Grace for your Waist*, Janelle Keith addresses the heart and some core issues facing our society today. I believe her honesty and vulnerability are a powerful tool God will use to speak to you. This book will stir your soul, put you face to face with some necessary questions, and peel back the lies you believe about yourself. She will help you personalize the truth of God's word in your life, all while continually point you to a loving Savior, Jesus Christ."
Cody Chaloner, Pastor, Life.Church, Stillwater, OK

Grace for Your Waist:
Living a Lifestyle Fitted with Hope

Janelle Keith

Woven Books
YOUR STORY. HIS GLORY.

...being confident of this very thing,
that He who has begun
a good work in you
will complete it
until the day
of Jesus Christ.

Philippians 1:6 (NKJV)

WITH GRATITUDE...

First and foremost, I desire to glorify God by acknowledging His sovereignty and His goodness. I'm at a loss at how to say my appreciation to the many encouragers who have contributed in my life.

Lori Clapper, my editor and friend, has been a huge support and one who was an "early believer" in my ability to write my story down. Not only has she lovingly massaged my story but brought a perspective which produced something excellent. I'll be indebted to her for walking alongside me.

Mr. Chad Robinson prophesied my voice to this "stage." As my spiritual mentor and counselor, he challenged me to develop an excellent story from a hope-filled perspective. His wife, Christie, pastored by example. I honor you with these hope-laden words of healing and wholeness over my life. There are too many pastoral and wellness influencers to list here, but please know I am forever grateful for the years that you've added to my life.

A special and deeply heartfelt gift of appreciation goes back to my immediate family. My husband, Terry, believed in me when I couldn't even give thought to how it was all going to turn out. My children, now grown, lived with me through this process. I'll admit it was miserable for them. But as a result, their support through the thick and thin counted as a win for us all. So, to Terry, Lindsay, and Shayne, I'll never forget how you helped me up each time I fell.

Although this book took years to come to life, I always received grace from my dear friend Tina Ahern who willingly stepped into my heart and pulled me out of my emotional depression. Her devotion to good health and nutrition completes my education and wellness story.

PREFACE

"Writing a novel is like driving a car at night. You can see only as far as your headlights, but you can make the whole trip that way."
- E.L. Doctorow

This quote was given to me on September 4, 2011, and I started writing this book on September 1, 2015. But my story started many years before that. I knew I was to write down my thoughts and believed help and healing could come through it. What I didn't realize was that laying out my heart on paper would result in such authenticity, accountability, and produce inner healing.

So, if anyone was changed in the composition of this book, it's the person behind the keys. This book is the fruit of my weight-loss journey—from start to today. I've lost half of my former self in more than one way. The number one question I'm asked is, "How did you do it?" I'm challenged to not only tell a good story but one where the very breadth and scope of my journey births life to another.

My purpose in this project is reconciliation and true hope. Stories are like seeds that either choose to die or push through the barriers and flourish. Each takes time to germinate, cultivate, yield, and produce. Every story matters and deserves a start. Your life is worthy of another examination. Earning space and owning issues are good measures to see value in the investment of personal character. Giving time to future growth blooms development, beauty, and maturity.

To seek healing and freedom is a process which requires trust. Empathy is a compassionate gift which captivates another with honesty and sincerity. My desire is to deposit a spark of change or curiosity through a perspective of good health and God's word. My prayer and hope are that you see yourself in these pages with anticipation of God's best for you.

"Now faith is the substance of things hoped for, the evidence of things not seen. For by it the elders obtained a good testimony. By faith, we understand that the worlds were framed by the word of God so that the things which are seen were not made of things which are visible." (Hebrews 11:1-3 NKJV)

Trust these words for yourself as you are led. Believe that God has you on this journey for a purpose of reconciliation and healing.

Each chapter was given by His order and release. I shuffled through a lot of words to get to this point. The process has changed me from the inside out; it's given my life a different perspective and completely flipped the script of my life.

I sincerely and fervently ask that you, too, take an honest look at your past and own it. Each chapter will challenge you and inspire you as we discuss different choices through stories of my own emotional suffering. A weight loss journey uncovers a variety of hidden issues awaiting a solution. It's in the discovery and resolution of some very personal heart issues, that I found my hope and freedom. And you can, too.

Janelle Keith

Introduction

Let's Get Started: What's in Your Closet?

Ah! A woman's closet! There's not a single place on earth that can

tell a woman's story better than her closet. It's a snapshot of her life, both current and past. For years, my closet has served as a prayer chamber, the place where I shared secrets (mainly with myself), my safe haven in troubled times, a refuge of peace and quiet, and even a place to sneak away for a quick nap when my children were toddlers. It's also served another purpose not quite as glamorous: a dreary collection of my personal failures and disappointments.

Welcome to My Closet

Exactly how did my closet constantly mock me? Let's start with an inventory of clothes to fit a 244-pound woman! There you go. I just courageously admitted one of my most guarded secrets: my heaviest weight, a.k.a. my "start" point. (If you have ever been on any weight loss plan, you know the term all too well.) It was a time when my closet served more as a voice of ridicule rather than a sacred haven. It was a dark and emotionally driven stage in my life.

Every time I entered my closet, not only was I reminded of my current situation, but I was discouraged by the increased task in front of me—to diet and lose weight. However, many attempts at various weight loss programs left me heavier physically, yet empty emotionally. I stepped back and looked into the recesses of many frustrations. What I saw revealed a wide menu of more failures than successes; more consumption of convenient meals over well-planned options; a collection of excuses rather than triumphs; more justifications for bad choices than disciplines to stay the course. My closet held a vicious cycle of unfulfilled resolutions. And I could never seem to break free.

I know, firsthand, what it's like to live through years of regret, rejections, misconceptions, and negativity about weight loss. And after many years of failed efforts, I also know the forgiveness for my bad choices and experienced freedom from the bondage of food. So if you will, allow me to sweep out those darkened corners of my closet and disclose how I arrived at the place where I was ready to change— not as a means to an end, but as a total lifestyle transformation forever.

It's no secret billions of people have dieted over the years. Their desks are stacked high with diet books as they search for the next gimmick to magically make those pesky pounds disappear…this time. Let me be the first to tell you: *This is not one of those books!* Factually, this isn't a diet plan at all, but a journey of how God called me to obedience and my response to His call.

This is my story of deliverance, redemption, and how simple obedience to God's Word allowed me to shed 132 pounds. The truth is you won't find hope in those dusty stacks of diet books, those worn out, food-stained recipe cards, in your empty New Year's resolutions and the very least, not in your wishful easy desires.

Hope doesn't live in disappointments, but it can thrive again. Perhaps you've had a measure of success with some diet plans but still have weight to lose. Maybe you've lost weight, but still struggle with self-esteem issues. You could be like millions of others who feel powerless to lose and keep off the pounds. Do you, like many, lack self-control and still deal with cravings? No matter where you fit on the spectrum of weight loss, this book will continually present a solution of hope.

Are you ready? Here's what you need to remember…

- ❖ My solution can work for you. I will share how God helped me out of bondage and set my mind back on track to follow Him on the right path of good health.
- ❖ You don't need another "YOU SHOULD" in your life. This book is a collection of heart stories and helps to get anyone to a place of freedom.
- ❖ Hard work is worth the effort, BUT sacrifice will cost you. Behavior changes are hard but doable.
- ❖ Ralph Waldo Emerson helped me to think better of myself. He wrote, "What lies behind us, and what lies before us are small matters compared to what lies within us." You *can* think better of yourself!

- ❖ This is a process of ownership in your life with the goal of victory over defeat. If you want to shed the issues and the fears which fuel bondage, perhaps it's time to allow God inside your "soul closet" to heal you.

❖ Commit to improve yourself; ask God to help you, and partner with God to achieve your best. You must *desire* God's best wardrobe.

Through it all, remember you don't need another diet plan, you need to love food less and love God more. I want you to win, and I believe in you. Furthermore, God cares about your soul health as well as the physical parts of you.

Now let me ask you, "What's in your closet?" This is more than a "how to" book; it's a book of action. Your weight loss journey will never get past square one with information only. You must desire change. At the end of each chapter you'll find action steps and a prayer. Do yourself a favor — take the time to engage in both. Action facilitates life-change! You aren't in this alone; I will walk you through your hidden issues as you take a closer look at mine. Remember: God is able AND there is hope. Welcome to your transformation.

Chapter 1

Looking for Love

My story may surprise you, but it didn't surprise God! He had it all planned out. Once I started my quest to find the real me, it became obvious He was next to me, constantly at work with His greater plan for my life. But to live the life He desired for me, I had to first lay down my will and put it all on the line.

In my search for love, significance, and acceptance, I came to the point where I had to ask God to break open the part of me which *should have* invited Him long ago. I sought Him for answers to questions which were on repeat in my mind since I was five years old. "Who am I and where do I belong?" At least, my heart only opens back as far as my mind will allow me to travel. This emotional place is where my moment of discovery really began—in the place where I felt the most inadequate, the most in need, the weakest…at my roots. Perhaps it's a good place to start your journey, too.

I was born on August (the eighth month) on the 8th day and weighed eight pounds, eight ounces. What a whole lot of eights lined up on one day! For years, the significance of these numbers never registered with me—until I came to understand the significance of Biblical numerology. All throughout the Bible, the number eight represents new beginnings. After the earth was destroyed by flood, eight people walked off the ark to begin life again. The Bible records eight accounts of people who rose from the dead. Elijah performed eight miracles. Jesus—the ultimate new beginning—arose on the first day of the week—the eighth day, and so on.

In my desperation to find myself in this world, I lost sight of my identity in Christ and my purpose for living. Oh, how I needed a new beginning. Sadly, I didn't realize my true identity until *much later* in life.

My closet opened up a memory hidden within my own family tree. I grew up the third child in a normal home, a healthy baby girl, the second daughter in our family. It's funny how often I've heard the word "healthy" in reference to a newborn's weight. In other people's mind, I was born healthy. In my mind, I was born fat and saw myself as overweight for years on end.

Let me say right now I wish I could jump into super hyper mode and take you to the very end of my story. A huge part of me wants to glaze over all the painful details and show you the hope I never saw when I was a fat baby, child, teenager, and adult. But if I skipped ahead, you would miss why I needed hope in the first place. This is where my healing begins.

The Cheetos Heroine

My day of reckoning really commenced when I was about five years old. Our family had just arrived at my cousin's house for a visit. As was normal, my grandmother set the boundaries where we could play and what was off limits. Within minutes, my older sister and two bookend cousins were arm and arm doing coveted "big girl" stuff. Like normal nine-year-old girls, the sounds of giggles, grins, and whispers filled the air. And much like how a dryer sheet sticks to a pair of double knit pants, they were inseparable. I watched them all squeeze through a skinny hallway as if their hips were conjoined at birth. Then, in a flash, they disappeared into their makeshift big girl command station—my cousin's bedroom.

Sadly, my sister's plan of escape from me was strategic. I say sad because I was immediately uninvited. I didn't want to rain on their parade, I only wanted to belong. I wanted to be included in their circle of big girl fun. My desire was to be accepted on their team and to be included in their lives. And I set my mind to do whatever it took. I simply wanted to fit in.

No matter how I begged, bargained, cajoled, and downright pleaded to be included, they never budged on their steadfast mission to keep me out. Even my promise to remain in my "sit quiet" pose in a corner produced no favorable permission. Finally, a crack in the door. Could this be the moment when my persistence paid off? Not exactly.

Fed up with my appeal, my pre-teen dominators responded, "Go away! Go play with your baby dolls. You're not old enough or smart enough to play with us. You won't understand the things we're talking about." Those were *their* "reasons," but my inner-critic voice heard: *"Go away! You're not thin enough to play with us!"*

Afterward, what seemed to take a lifetime, it happened. Hunger broke out among the troops. It was my time to shine and to throw them my best beg. I would show I could be the invisible little sister. The door cracked and out flew a flat leather play purse. Yes! The olive branch. Now, it was my opportunity to prove myself worthy of inclusion into their sorority! My sister ordered me to journey into forbidden territory—the snack sanctuary—where grandma hid the giant glass jar of Cheetos. *Mmmmm,* Cheetos. The forbidden fruit! What better place for grandma to stash them than on top of her refrigerator! It was now my chance to earn their approval. I knew I could do this!

While the sequestered gigglers stayed in their element—content with bouncing boy stories between themselves—I set out to accomplish my mission with a quiet attitude in check. This was my chance to risk it all and to claim my spot. I was confident once I put myself on the line, I would belong, I would be accepted, I would be one of them, and I would finally be happy.

It seemed so easy in my mind. All I had to do was take one small risk. Those Cheetos had my name written all over them. Using my super-ninja-snack-sneaking skills, I spotted the prize on top of the mountainous refrigerator in a glass jug. YUM, those orange puffs were alive! They taunted and had such a brilliant powdery golden glow. How could an object so full of promise be "off limits?" Now, within my grasp, my course of action was obvious. Simply scale the kitchen table, grab the prize, fill the purse, and return with the spoils. Then, I would be in like Flynn! *(Whoever Flynn is, I wanted to be IN like him!)* My trump card, dutifully earned, would be accepted at the door.

Without eye or ear detection, I successfully loaded what seemed to be a bottomless bag full of puffed cheesy curls. There was no time to stop and even taste the prize. With the strength of a warrior champion, I scaled down the chair and tip-toed through the hallway, with the clutched treasure in my white-knuckled fist. I could hear the motherly chatter like magpies in the front room, a good sign as they were too busy to notice me! Now, the moment of truth. Award time!

I arrived at the sacred door of community with the prize in hand. My perceived inclusion was imminent. Just then, the door cracked open ever so slightly. My moment of acceptance had arrived. Like a flash of lightning, my sister's slender arm jutted through the thin opening, she forcefully grabbed the leather-bound bag with brute strength. There I stood—speechless. Never did I anticipate what immediately followed—the door, along with a ton of disappointment, quickly slammed in my face. From the other side of rejection, I could hear munches from the bounty retrieved at my own risk. Their laughter grew louder and stronger as they celebrated the win . . . but without me.

It happened so fast! Here I was brave enough to perform such a dangerous and heroic act. What more could I have done? My agenda was specific, strategic, and executed to perfection. My accomplishments didn't gain my sister's approval. The truth was now painfully obvious: I was never their Cheetos heroine; I was only their snack mule.

My next move was just as strategic. I headed straight to mom. I was the biggest tattle tale in history, complete with tears like waterworks over the regret of my behavior. The wrath of my mother for my actions still makes me wince a little. I wasn't labeled a hero. Instead from that day forward I wore another label: *loser*.

The Truth About Lies

The problem with labels is they are sticky and attach themselves to stereotypes. From the Cheetos moment, I realized my flesh craved approval, acceptance, and place to call home . . . even within my own family. Labels like "tag-along", "runt", "forgotten", "couldn't tie her own shoes", "unhealthy", "fat" child, etc. stuck to me and irritated like a scratchy tag in my identity. I eventually did find my place of recognition and self-significance in just about any food group packaged to please my flesh: Little Debbie's cakes, peanut M & M's, Twinkies, chips, cookies, and cheese. It ALL stuck hard to my heart and my hips.

Surely, I'm not the only one who's ever been down this path. Wasn't this Eve's story, as well? Didn't she want to belong? Didn't she swallow the first lie of deception the enemy dished out? Didn't she trust her own rationale over the God who had just formed her from the very rib of man? Wasn't she attracted by the allure of attention and acceptance? Yes, yes, yes, and yes.

From the start of life on this earth until today, everyone is in search of themselves, a purpose for life and happiness. The truth is we are looking for what only God can fill. We want to belong, and we have the need to be loved. How hard we fall to the twisted truth and seductive voice which tells us our happiness is found in the gain of "things" over the loss of ourselves. It's a lie. The serpent offered Eve the same empty promise. Eve took the bait and fell . . . hard. Through each fallen life forward, mankind has been cursed with a defective bloodline—an inheritance of iniquity.

No matter how long or where *I* searched for acceptance and fulfillment, it evaded me. My young, innocent heart was continually bombarded with lies that provoked my personal pursuit of happiness.

Over and over again, they invaded and crushed my life at the most opportune times, especially at the height of my search for a false sense of approval. Still, I searched.

For the Love

In 1980, country singer Johnny Lee topped the charts with his smash hit, *Looking for Love*. People by the millions identified with the anthem as they, too, found themselves "Looking for love in all the wrong places!" I was one of them. And this is what I found to be true.

When you are out on a limb desperately seeking approval, you position yourself for failure in the search for love. Before you know it, you become a starving pauper who spends your life looking on every shelf, only to find pleasures which can never reciprocate the depth of love you seek. This may sound extreme, but when you're enslaved and desirous, you are attracted to all the wrong places until you find what gives you satisfaction.

I was on a journey to find real love. I looked high, low, long, and hard—anywhere and everywhere, tasted hidden pleasures along the way. I searched and searched for as many nods of affirmation as an impoverished child could consume. It wasn't long before I became a slave to the journey.

Every little girl wants to hear she's pretty, especially from their father. But, I never heard these words from *my earthly father*. At no time do I remember him expressing his love or showing it in a way a child could grasp. Therefore, I didn't mature with a close-knit father's love. It seemed (to me) his love was distant, cold, and hard to earn. What was obvious was how he showered his love on my older brother and sister (at least in my mind). Maybe he felt it was unnecessary as he proved his love through other ways such as his provision and care. His absence of affirmation was detrimental to my soul. Perhaps this is a generational attitude, but even so, no little girl should feel such shame for an emotion she can't see or feel.

A father's affirmation means the most; it's the way children see and receive acceptance. A father speaks to the identity needs in boys and reaffirms the love needs in daughters.

In retrospect, this was the real root of my unquenchable thirst for approval. Since I never knew true acceptance by paternal love, it left me clueless, which resulted in an unclear identity. I spent years living with buried hidden issues full of cream-filled regrets. Thus, another label stuck to my soul: uninvited. Where would I ever find my *real place*?

The Change

Due to comparison and perceived favoritism, I was uninvited most of my childhood. And on the other hand, I continued to look for what I thought I could never have. I wasted a lot of time in competition with others. I turned to food to comfort me and soften life's rejection blows. Lots and lots of food.

But at my core, it was never a food issue, but rather a heart issue. My wounded heart sought validation from food, people, money, significance, status, position, etc. The truth is, every time I met someone— even far into my adult years—it seemed as though my initial introduction was, "Hi. I'm Janelle and I want you to like me!" My life was miserable...and when a miserable person copes with hidden issues, the coping mechanism itself becomes the best comfort! I found that food doesn't measure, compare, nor talk back! AND *misery LOVES company*. Until my "someday" became THE day I changed closets!

No approval can match what our Creator has to offer.

After many years of frustration and emptiness, I finally walked out of my closet of despair and into the closet of God's grace! Here, I found a realization that initiated my turnaround. "No approval can match what our Creator has to offer, and God can't bless who you pretend to be!" – Steven Furtick

The truth is: hidden issues plague us all! We ALL have our stuff. Whether it's the serpent of Cheetos, forbidden fruits, self-pleasures, approval ratings, number of friends, or empty promises, they only offer a false perception of what God originally intended for us to enjoy. Happiness, approval, acceptance, and love can only be found in God who gives it to us freely and in the purest form. Christian author, C.S. Lewis, described it so beautifully: "Don't let your happiness depend on something you may lose... only (upon) the Beloved who will never pass away."

It was in my closet, my prayer closet (where I am closest to God), where I found the healing I so desperately desired—**rest** for my broken heart. Hidden under God's lens of truth, He led me to a place of healing from the inside out. I quickly came to realize the acceptance I had spent my life yearning for in the label of "Love." God, my Heavenly Father, has already provided it through His Son, Jesus. It was just my job to receive and accept it.

My history is full of falls like Humpty Dumpty off the walls around my heart. I didn't understand why I couldn't put myself back together again. My life was in pieces until I allowed God to reconfigure my emotional puzzle and reprogram my mind.

In many fractured and feeble attempts to fix me, I realized only God could put me back together again. When my heart lined up with His heart for me, I found the authentic intimacy I craved.

Making It Real

As you can tell, my story isn't just about weight loss. My overall life change took years to accomplish. With my true identity hidden in Christ, true freedom allowed me to not only shed the weight I had accumulated, but purged my closet of the chewed-up self-esteem and broken ego. On the outside, people might have thought I had it all together. It appeared I was confident and knew my identity. After all, I was their voice on a Christian radio station, and was their "go-to" God girl for prayer and encouragement. The broken part of me was hidden well, like those extra pounds I wanted to cover up. I wanted that part of me to disappear on its own.

We have fears and hidden junk in our closets. I had to get real with myself and uncover the truth. It was then I allowed God to heal me, deliver me, and re-purpose my closet space.

No matter how spiffed up and pretty you are in front of your friends, the real you lies beneath what everyone can see. We all would like to believe we control our lives. We don't. Yes, we love to strut our stuff, but there is "the thing beneath the thing beneath the thing." Or in other words, our past begs reconciliation from the inside out from our inner being of heart, soul, and mind. The answers and affirmations we seek are only found in one place—God!

In this day and age, we have solutions to many issues. Still, there are no easy remedies for the problem of obesity. There is only one place of real hope—a place of refuge to satisfy the heart's deepest desires. We have a God who cares about every little pound we fight. We have an advocate at work on our behalf. We have a heavenly Father who is *not blind to our struggles* but provides a way out of every temptation we face. We have a hope!

Let me encourage you. Weight loss isn't rocket science. It's actually as easy as you desire it to be. Change happens when you put your self-control on the line. Whether you have 10 or 400 pounds to lose, it's all an extension of an underlying heart issue—those hardened parts of your life ruled by an appetite for comfort, pleasure, or even further…I'll let you fill in your own blank. When you give God complete control and lay down your will on the altar, you must submit to His ways. Then your inner wounds are healed and the true battles with "self" are won.

Before we go any further, I want you to be honest with yourself for a moment. Take a look at the real you…the hurting part which longs to be accepted at your current weight. Where do you run when life doesn't go your way? Where does your mind drift? If you're like me, it's straight to chocolate! What are you hiding from?

God knows the real you. He knows you and what you are running from. The truth is, ignorance of your hidden issues will remain until you make peace with them. No matter how you've lived, or accumulated stuff, or accomplished goals, hidden issues stay hidden until you dig deep. Even if your body looks good, you will always wonder about the real you…until you make peace with yourself.

The answer lies within you. Take a look at your issues, whether small or large, and this lens will help free you from what has kept you prisoner. God wants you healed, but hidden issues cause dysfunction in your life. Lies and deceit keep you from an intimate relationship with God and others, in a real and vulnerable way. It's time to put down the masks and get real. Put a stop to your dysfunctional relationships forever. No more expenditure of your time and energy on useless quests for happiness, which will never be resolved outside the love of your Heavenly Father. This is the end of your search . . .

. . . And the beginning of your new life.

Think About It

1. When you don't feel as though you measure up to the world's standards, what brings you comfort — or what is your escape?

2. What would it take for you to be the person physically, mentally, emotionally, and spiritually you want to be?

3. Where in your life have you swallowed a lie or worn a label for your place in this world, and tucked it away in your closet?

Kickstart Action Steps

Grab your journal or a piece of paper and write out this promise from Psalm 37:3-5: "Trust in the Lord, and do good; dwell in the land and befriend faithfulness. Delight yourself in the Lord, and he will give you the desires of your heart. Commit your way to the Lord; trust in him, and he will act." Now post this promise in your "closet."

Prayer

God, I need Your help in clothing my image. Set me free. The world has twisted my perspective from a pure and holy image into a plastic coated, sugar dipped, chocolate-laden, fancy comfort to me. Take me back to the garden of Your goodness, and show me how I am to look, appear, and shine.

I need help. You, Father, love me and want to perfect Your work in me. Please help me to be real and honest in Your presence and search the closet of my heart. Do not forsake the work of Your hands, and let me not fall to excuses or escape again. Keep me from temptation and show me a way out. Remind me of Your hope and future for me. Your intentions are good for me. I want to live a life of purity and good health when it comes to nutrition. I thank You for your cleansing work. In Jesus' name. Amen.

Notes

Chapter 2

The Walk-In Closet: Labels to Lies

𝒥 don't know about you, but I *love* walk-in closets! They are so big and roomy and hold so many stunning outfits. For me, the bigger the closet the better. Oh, how I love walking into that huge space specifically designated for rows and rows of tops, pants, blazers, skirts, dresses, shoes . . . and more shoes . . . and more shoes. Walk-in closets are the best! Or are they?

While I absolutely love them now, the "walk-in closet" of my life hasn't been nearly as exciting and inviting. For years, it was a dark place for me to hide my deepest insecurities and hurts behind whatever label of comfort and healing I could find. In doing so, I advanced to a size 22! So many hurts, so much pain, so many labels. These are a few of them.

Label: Plain and Plaid

I will always distinctly remember how my mother dressed me for my first-grade pictures—in plaid. Now, nothing screams "fat" in a child's mind like plaid! And with my self-esteem already in the tank, I didn't need any help feeling unworthy. But somehow, plaid was one of my first labels that helped mask my true identity.

Every Christmas, my grandmother supported my need for plaid by encouraging my ever-growing collection in my closet. That was okay by me, as I thought that's what fat girls wore. Growing up, I got to sit on her big old couch and leaf through the Sears and Roebuck Catalog, only circling the dresses that were many pages *after* the skinny style—a special sizing for chubby girls like me. I didn't realize that I was already resigning to being heavy. I didn't realize I was wearing a plain label or even a negative one. My desire was to simply fit in with my skinny friends, just opting for what fit me best in the "healthy" styles. Isn't it funny that the clothes in our closets label us before we even know it?

Our inner confidence is built on our perceptions of our reality, and we begin to view everything through that "reality." Our self-confidence becomes the most important comfort we can give ourselves. So much so that we eventually resign to the theory that if we have to be fat, we might as well look good.

We all endure growing pains throughout childhood years, but I never imagined my heart could be driven to such hurtful places at such a young age. But pain is sometimes our best teacher in that our response truly formulates our ideas, thoughts, and feelings. However, if we're not careful, pain can cause our feelings to become dictators of our actions instead of indicators of our situation. Sadly, I fell prey to this trap.

Label: Abandoned

My early school years were tough. You wouldn't think so, seeing that my mom was the cook at my private grade school; and unlike most kids I felt insecure even though I knew home was only a half block away. How well I remember my first day of kindergarten. Mom walked me to my class and then turned to leave. Just then, I blurted out from my little insecure heart, "No! Don't go mommy!" That day, my plaid dress caught my waterfall of tears.

My kindergarten teacher had a big job ahead of her—cutting me away from my mom's apron strings. She gently pulled me into the classroom that day, not realizing this would be an everyday occurrence. Each day, Mom dropped me off, and again she would turn around and leave. When she did, waves of abandonment flooded my little five-year-old soul.

As I watched mom walk down that long hallway, it seemed that she was so out of touch with my feelings. My insecurities could not stay silent. Couldn't she hear me crying? If I screamed louder, would she turn around and come back? Why was she abandoning me, knowing I would be afraid of everyone in my class? Would I ever see her again or was she actually leaving me for good? Such a big bundle of emotions from such a small heart. Little did I know, Mom was doing what every good mom does: giving me space to be independent. But my label of abandonment wouldn't allow me to see it that way.

Later in life, I learned the truth about my early school days: My mom was just as heartbroken as I was. Many years later from her aged recliner, she admitted, "Janelle, it was all I could do to walk away and leave you standing there. But I knew it was the best for you." I knew she was right, seeing that she had experienced the horror of abandonment at a young age herself.

As a child, my mom suffered with polio. This was many years before there was a vaccination to help prevent such an awful disease. At the age of nine, she was completely disconnected from her family for almost a year to endure treatments. What a nightmare for a child. What an agony for a mom—to see her child suffer and to be separated in her time of misery. I truly believe that the real tragedy wasn't only my mom's illness, but the loneliness she felt in the separation. Little did I know that she knew exactly how I felt watching her walk away those days, yet she did it for my good. It seemed like torture then, but today, I'm thankful.

Label: Orphaned

I've heard it said many times that the worst loneliness in the world is being lonely in a crowd. In the same way, the worst childhood is having a biological family, yet feeling like an orphan the entire time. Such was my life.

Just as every little girl desires, I wanted to have one-on-one time with my mother so badly, but she was always working. The only time we spent, just us, was at the kitchen sink watching birds while we did the dishes together. No mother-daughter talks, no mommy-daughter date nights, no weekends away. Only birds and dishes. I followed her to work many times just to spend time with her. If we ever did have any time together, it was always when she was doing another task, as if I was invisible.

My mom did the best she could, working three jobs while I was in high school. I watched her sweat out a partial income for our family, but she constantly gave everything away. She made everyone feel special, like they were her favorites. I loved her devotion and admired her love of people.

Much like my relationship with my mom, my Dad and I never had daddy-daughter time because he was always working, as well. Dad was one to show his "love" through money. One time, I assumed he was showing his love for me as he offered to pay me a dollar for every pound I lost! That *sounds* like a good motivation to lose some weight, right? Wrong. Instead of seeing it as an incentive or an act of love, my label twisted his motives and I swallowed the lie that love had to be bought. I don't remember receiving any dollars that summer . . . or any other summer for that matter.

Both of my parents passed away in 2016, and it took until the end of their days for me to see that they loved me in their own respective ways. My dad wasn't expressive, as most men aren't. My mom became very expressive in her later years. I truly believe the biggest domestic abuse is against ourselves in that we fail to see the many ways that love *can* be expressed without words.

I missed a deep-seated kind of love due to a wounded heart and thus opened up to a label of emotional ignorance. With that hovering over my life, I failed to see my significance. Every night I cried out loudly from my bedroom bunk, "I love you!" But only silence in return. Not even the crickets would respond. The absence of that verbal affirmation—from the people I needed it from the most—did deep damage.

One casualty was my self-assurance. I failed to gain confidence in knowing that my life mattered. Then, I didn't have a skinny or confident leg to stand on. I always felt like the "red-headed step child" even though I was neither red headed nor a stepchild. My brother used to joke that I was adopted. I secretly believed him. It didn't matter to my selfish thoughts. That's how I felt. I didn't know the love of my Heavenly Papa, and my heart was far from receiving the love He readily had for me.

Little did my parents know that my esteem, or lack thereof, was attached to the number of times they said, "I love you"—which I can count on one hand. Thus, the lie that I wasn't good enough to be loved—a.k.a. an orphan spirit—was planted deep within my soul. So deep that it annihilated my self-worth. Instead of showers of positive affirmations, my mind was constantly flooded with words like: unwanted, unloved, unworthy, unapproved, uninvited, unknown, unheard, misunderstood, and just about every other "un" word you could think of.

This might sound incredibly selfish. However, every child needs positive affirmations and attention. If it doesn't come from parents, the world will fill the attention deficit need. I'm sure my parents were doing the best they could, but it felt as if I only got the leftovers of them, which left my heart empty. I convinced myself I was unworthy of love. A lie from Satan himself.

I assumed that my older brother—my parent's favorite—and my older sister—the smart one—got the best parts of my parents. That left me fighting for the crumbs off the table, the bits and pieces that were left up for grabs. This is what I thought I deserved mainly because I was the fat child. My formative years included typical sibling rivalry gone wrong in my mind.

Label: Rejected

When I was in grade school, there was the cutest girl in my class. She was pretty, skinny, popular, and certainly the coolest kitty around. This girl was everyone's friend . . . except mine. She even had an older sister who showed her the ropes on how to succeed in this thing called life. Her model of success and popularity became my grade school idol. My personal vow was to be her and wear her label of pretty, popular, and cool.

In the midst of searching for her secrets of success, I traced her coolness back to her hair—her trouble-free, shiny, thick, blonde, perfect hair! Never did I see one strand of hair out of place, whether at school, church, the mall, you name it. Even in our grade school track meets, it was tied in a pretty bow, never left its boundaries, and bounced perfectly at the nape of her neck. Then, when I looked in the mirror. . .

My hair? Well, it was just like the rest of me: dark, thick, unmanageable, problematic, embarrassing, and unruly. Since it was super straight, Mom decided my best look was to rock a pixie cut with the option of bangs. In the end, I resembled a boy most of my school days. I hated it as much as I did myself.

In the popularity contest—not to mention the cool, pretty, talented, and accepted contests—I was dead last. Even so, I set my expectations for acceptance on the highest bar and hung my heart on the unrealistic labels that spoke comparison, discouragement, and unacceptance. In the end, the over-played reality of rejection caused me to constantly hit repeat in my mind's recorder. I believed it all. *"Would I ever belong?"* and *"Will I ever be accepted as me?"*

Label: Insecure

We hide dysfunctions with labels in our walk-in closets, don't we? At one time I wore many of these, and it didn't take long for those to become my reality—in my mind at least. But most things are not what they seem!

Albert Einstein said, "Reality is merely an illusion, albeit a very persistent one." English author, Douglas Adams, added more revelation when he said, "Everything you see or hear or experience in any way at all is specific to you. You create a universe by perceiving it, so everything in the universe you perceive is specific to you." I lived in both worlds.

Since the days of plaid, my reality of my size was no more than a distorted perception. It wasn't long before my fat personality formed a severely bruised ego, which would live with me the rest of my life. It started early and escalated from there.

Fast-forward to the very awkward years known as junior high. They say it's the time of life where you live on the corner of safe and awkward. Yep, they were right in every possible way. Gone were the playground memories of being picked last for sporting events or the target for dodge-ball. Junior high was about boys, popularity, and pep club.

Sadly, I fell into the deception as every other junior higher—to not be the real me, but blend into the sea of purposeless faces. I tried squeezing my bruised ego into an overcrowded world of others doing the same. For me, it was mostly about my awkward, pimply, plain self. How I stood out—was with all my unique flaws.

This was my time where I felt invisible again. I disappeared and fell silent in my fight. I succumbed to the place of cheering for others who succeeded in life, those who made the grade. I felt left out, left behind, and missed the game on the sidelines. I was so afraid of ridicule and shame. If I came out of my closet in my size 16, tent-sized dresses, I was surely subject to further rejection. But what else was there? After all, rejection had already established its stronghold in my life years before. So I hid behind my smile, more pleats and plaid skirts, and straight boy-like bangs.

There was obviously something wrong with me that made me seem unacceptable to the boys my age. I was never asked to my junior or senior prom, so I went with two girlfriends! I tried everything I could think of to fill my void of security and significance—even faking humor about myself to others. Little did I realize that my humor was only sabotaging my identity. My friends joined in throwing jabs, as well. I never knew how much inner damage all of this "humor" was doing until years later. By the time high school ended, my self-worth was destroyed and I had nothing to hold on to.

Fortunately, I made it out of those awkward years, even though I looked like a boy most of the time. Wow, do I remember those hairstyles in that day! What was I thinking? It certainly wasn't style; it was a cover-up. I grew out my bangs and then swept them to the side to look cool . . . or to really cover my low self-esteem and hungry heart for acceptance.

Label: Unloved

Junior high came and went. Then the big leagues: high school! When I realized I couldn't compete in school academics, athletics, vocals, band, or life for that matter, I turned to something I knew I could do well: the school newspaper. It was there I wrote an advice column called "Dear Nellie." Can you guess the picture I used at the top of every piece of advice? Borden's Elsie the cow! Of course, it was my column's logo. How fitting!

The format was simple: students would write in their questions and "Nellie" would answer. The journalism department sold my advice for a penny a copy in the high school lobby during the lunch hour. The articles were a hit, but there was one caveat that no one ever knew: No one ever wrote in! All of the letters I replied to were actually my own personal questions about love, boys, and all things high school. Yes, every article was interesting, *but it was all fake.*

I remember thinking, *if no one is asking about love, then maybe they already found all the love they need.* Of course, then the label of "unloved" took over in my mind. I thought I was the only one in the entire school still looking for a steady love.

Each person that has ever walked on this planet is created with a void. It's the innate desire, placed in us by God, to have our love tanks filled. Many travel down extreme paths to fill that hole, only to finally realize that nothing or no one can fill it except the One who created it—God! Any other attempts are fake, twisted, counterfeit versions of love instead of the pure love of the Father. What I found is that His love can never be measured in plaid. In fact, it can't be measured at all.

Label: Shame

Enter the college years—the time when I was just looking to leave behind the life I had built for myself. Like every 18-year-old, I thought I had things figured out. How quickly I came to realize that I didn't! In the years following, I abandoned my own hopes and dreams of fitting in, which paved the way for some really poor choices—mentally, physically, emotionally, and spiritually.

Before attending college, I never knew what "the freshman 15" meant. But it didn't take me long to not only understand, but participate. Yes, I indeed excelled in that subject—quickly exceeded my all-time personal heaviest weight. But, it's college. Everyone—especially girls—experiences this kind of peer pressure as a freshman, right? It sounds like a good reason, but it was really nothing more than a safety net and a place to hide my puny excuses. Benjamin Franklin gave great advice when he said "People willing to trade their freedom for temporary security deserve neither and will lose both."

Instead of hammering the books at the library (like I told my parents), I was consumed with studying everyone else's insecurities. Whether in class, at the library, at the bar, in the club, it didn't matter the location—people's behaviors were my focus. Of course, I never looked at my own baggage! It was easier to sit on the front row and judge others. Then, I came up with a brilliant idea: The best way to fix myself was to give what I had left to those who needed it!

The next four years, I convinced myself that I could help people in their search for love and acceptance. I reasoned that with my compassion and life-experience, people would find me acceptable. But, the problem was my perception of reality was still skewed. Suffice to say, I wanted to give everyone else their answer instead of letting God fix me first, and then offering a true picture of hope. Thus, I never properly dealt with the missing pieces of my heart issues. In reality, I didn't really want to help anyone. This was yet another mere ploy for acceptance and popularity.

All through college, I gave into whatever would hold my voracious appetite for approval. All I wanted was real love—the "silent love" I never experienced as a child. Consequently, my actions sprung from my deep need and void. Therefore, I wound up letting go of my morals in order to live a new, unhindered life. I was free as a bird, out from underneath my parent's rule. I was attempting to own my life so I was determined to live it as *I* wanted. In the process, I sold my soul to pleasures which only revealed the deeper issues that never graduated from kindergarten.

So many summers I came home from college bearing a label of shame (along with piles of dirty laundry) and more extra pounds from my pleasure binges. Every fall, I enrolled with new motivations to make it the year of change, but quickly lost my resolve. I was living a duplicitous life full of guilt and shame. Here's what I came to realize: Shame and guilt trap you to wear labels that can only be broken by forgiveness in Christ.

My Refuge

Have you ever stopped to think about how our past shapes us into the people we are today? Those childhood labels seem to stick to us like tags from a retail shop. They never seem to let go! My past defined me with a defeatist attitude: I would always be forever fat, forever plain, forever abandoned, forever orphaned, forever rejected, forever shameful, and certainly not forever perfect. How I so desperately needed a friend who could provide comfort for my obliterated soul. I found it: food. And I fell deeply in love with it.

You can never erase the pain in your life by attaching your feelings to something false.

Let's be honest. Don't we all look for comfort especially in times of desperation? Aren't we all looking for something to make our pain go away? Don't we find ways to self-medicate and then replicate to cover up our pain? Once we find this soothing source, we attach ourselves to the point of over-indulgence. You know the answers as well as I do. It's part of our nature.

My love for comfort food never produced the results I desired. No matter how much I tried—or ate—my desperate craving for inner satisfaction could never be filled by a cheap substitution. Don't get me wrong, I loved food. But it never loved me back! Only God could produce what I yearned for, but that didn't stop me from hunting.

As my consumption of food increased, I soon came to a stark realization: the more weight I gained, the more food I desired! That seems crazy, but it's the truth. Eventually, my desires gave way to full out, whole-hearted devotion . . . then obsession. This wasn't like giving birth to a child—soon forgetting the intense pain as we hold our own in our arms. No, this marked my life. And I was blind to it.

No matter where you are on your journey, here's something to always remember: *You can never erase the pain in your life by attaching your feelings to something false.* How you handle your crises can be costly, even setting a trajectory of heartbreak for your future. Don't fall into the temptation, like millions of others, and label yourself as a victim. It's a trap that can keep you imprisoned for the rest of your life. But, you don't have to live in that prison!

Making It Real

After many years, I realized that it wasn't about my bad haircuts or my weight. Neither was it about the not-so-perfect complexion of my face or the perky smile that used to disappear with daily reflection. It's not about my opinion of myself or man's acceptance of me; it's about knowing that I am loved by a Holy God who can handle my eight-year-old disappointments from the playground of life! When you realize you're created as a carbon copy of God, feelings of rejection and unacceptance fade away.

The space in my walk-in closet held many disappointments. There hung the labels of "wounded" and "worthless." I was lost in that land of man's approval. ***But not now!*** God has closed those doors forever! Never will I let my heart return to a place that God has shut. Now God has labeled me "approved" and "worthy!"

Isaiah 62:3 says: "You shall also be a crown of glory in the hand of the Lord, and a royal diadem in the hand of your God." (NKJV) A diadem is defined as a "royal dignity or authority; a crown or a royal crown!" Now that's an accessory I'd love to wear–I've always wanted my own tiara!

Friend, the world is ready to label you. But, so is your Heavenly Father. When Jesus sets us free from our past labels, we become custom fit for the labels God has designed for us to wear! I found my identity, shaped by my past, in every corner, crevice, and cranny of my walk-in closet. It took a holy jolt for me to see the truth! Through the empowerment of the Holy Spirit, I began to turn my eyes from my defeated, dejected, oppressive self, to see what God had for my life. At times, I've had to do a double take! His design for me (and you) is nothing short of remarkable.

The truth is, you've carried these false labels around for far too long. It's time to cut these labels out of your life and step in God's closet. There you will find two new labels: "Forgiven" and "Freedom!" To accept yourself how God sees you will require laying down your pride and humbly coming before God in a most gut-wrenching and vulnerable way. It's hard. It's uncomfortable. It's embarrassing at times. But it's oh, so rewarding.

Every season or transition in my life, I put my emotions on the playground—measuring myself according to man's standards. For years, in times of stress and crisis, I looked to sweets to be my savior. Thank God, that pattern has now been broken.

All those years auditioning for social acceptance only left me void of my real identity. What I traded along the way was my sense of consequence regarding food and behavioral choices. Thus, I lived an unhealthy lifestyle fueled by unbalanced emotions and childhood labels. But, those days are over.

Once I found the truth of who I am in Christ, the lies concerning love I swallowed as a child proved to be a false representation of true love—God's love! The love of God is full, complete, boundless, and extravagant. No other love compares to His richness in mercy and grace. No longer are we orphans, but sons and daughters of the Most High God!

Nothing compares to Him. His love is without rival! Today, I have a new walk-in closet with a whole new outlook!

Think About It

1. What labels from your childhood have stuck to your soul?

2. What lies or excuses have you attached to your self-worth?

3. What changes can you make to see yourself as God sees you?

Kickstart Action Steps

Completely read Psalm 139. And then read it again. Memorize it if you can. Let it settle in your mind, heart, and soul. See how David—a man who wore many labels yet measured up among all men—even expressed real concerns with God concerning his existence. Allow David's response to God help you clear any labels from your past and accept the truth about God's deep love for you. Now, write a prayer of forgiveness for yourself and admit that God loves you the same as you were many labels ago.

Prayer

God, I look to You alone for approval. I need Your help in changing the way I see myself. Your Word says I am fearfully and wonderfully made. Your very breath breathes in me, stripping away the unlovely things I think about myself. Teach me to love me the way You love me, despite all my flaws and failures. Remind me that in Christ I am now free, forgiven, and faultless. Renew my mind with Your label of holiness. Empower me to bravely live in my new label: **WHOLE!** Thank You for the holy work that You are doing in my life today. In Jesus' name, Amen.

Notes

Chapter 3
Toss It Out!

Welcome to my exposed closet where I wave my uncomfortable

underwear! Honestly, I would like to skip this chapter because I'm not proud of how I lived my life. But my story, like everyone's, is *my* story—the good, bad, and the ugly.

At this point, after the last chapter, my life's story probably looks like a large cluttered closet with pent up hurts and emotional baggage. My years of over-indulged emotional baggage left my shoulders worn and ragged. But, I was so comfortable with my baggage full of ill-fitting emotions and fear of change, I couldn't see a way out. The summation of my life, up until the end of college, was dinged up, faded, and certainly dingy. But, my journey continued . . . complete with all the baggage.

My Duplicitous Life

I graduated college with a degree in Social Sciences, with an emphasis in social work. In the art of relationships, it's important to note I missed all the signs of my own emotional scars, fears, and hurts. However, I thought if I spent my life helping others grapple with their issues, it would somehow help me wrestle with my own. I loved the idea of leading people to see how change could empower them but failed to love myself on the same level of compassion.

I started to realize how comfortable it was to look at other's problems while I lived in ignorance of my own. In my mind, I thought my life was beyond change. I rationalized, "Hey, at least I'm helping somebody, right?"

Here's the truth I came to learn: To effectively help others, God must first fix the issues within us. Once healed, a testimony can be used to bring healing to others. **You can't give away what you don't first possess.**

Isn't it funny how we can accept our issues, while at the same time not show any tolerance of those same areas in someone else? The Bible calls it hypocrisy. Now, it's getting uncomfortable! Hang on. This gets better.

As people with Christian consciences, we cannot nor should not approve of everything we are or do. For example, for years I spoke negative words over my life and just accepted them as part of my makeup. I also believed I had plenty of time "for God to fix me later." Then, there was another side of me—mainly, my weight and health— which I thought God didn't care about at all. Controlled by a victim mentality, I did a horrible job of managing my health in college. God didn't care about it, so why should I? Thus, I gave into all kinds of temptations and flirtations with danger.

I took wild rides on the same merry-go-round for years and began to ask myself, "The problem couldn't be me, could it? Surely, there was someone . . . anyone . . . to blame for the way I let myself go to ruin, right?" Boy, was I in for a rude awakening when I discovered the harsh truth: We are products of our environment, but only to a degree.

Yes, we have the power of choice to counter-balance our behaviors; the intelligence to adapt to our exposure; and the power of reason to make moral choices based on possible future outcome. But, sometimes we do not always *employ* the power of reason and must live with the physical or emotional outcome of a bad decision. The truth is, even though we often believe we are victims of circumstance, we choose our paths in life. And there was one decision I was very proud to make.

Blooming

While working at a local manufacturing plant after college, I met a man named Terry. Oh, how I loved his blonde hair, swooped by his charisma. It was his gentle spirit of acceptance that hooked me. In my drive to gain his attention, I lost weight to seal the deal! As we got to know each other better, Terry began to love me like no man ever did— which I missed from my father. He loved me in spite of my past and paid no attention to my numerous battles with the bulge. It wasn't long before we were married . . . and then life really started.

After we were married, two things began to blossom: our love for each other and my weight! Like all young married couples, we ate at home. And we ate well. *Good Housekeeping* taught me that a good husband needed a full tank! Terry grew up on potatoes and a double portion of gravy. So, I knew the way to reach him was through his stomach—one homemade pizza at a time, each one thickly coated with melted cheese. My down home culinary skills definitely won him over, but I paid the price as my weight dutifully blossomed.

Three years after we were married, I gave birth to our first child, Lindsay. Now, I bloomed into motherhood for the first time. While pregnant with Lindsay, I gained 60 pounds. Of course, I used every excuse from the motherhood book. After all, I was eating for two! However, baby permission didn't negate my drive to stay healthy as I remained in pretty good shape while I carried my first born. I even walked four miles the day she came into the world! Then came the delivery. After Lindsay was born, I knew the rules of health; I just didn't stick to them. And I reaped the consequences.

Pushing myself to gain control, I enrolled in a local weight-loss group to take off some added pounds, which somehow found their way to my thighs. I was ready to jump in, push those weights, run those laps, and shed the weight like no one's business. But it didn't work quite so easy. The start was small, the progress was slow, but finally . . . finally. . . I reached my target weight of 110 pounds. Time to celebrate! Success lasted a day before I fell off track.

I could feel my emotions warring against my common sense. But nothing says, "I appreciate your hard work as a mom," any better than a package of Peanut M & M's! You're familiar with the chocolaty goodness which surrounds the peanuts, with those fun colored candy shells. It's yummy-ness in a small yellow bag, and thus my reward for mothering my daughter. And my long stay-at-home-mom day became sweeter because of that yellow bag . . . and the 200 calories inside.

The yellow bag soon gave way into other dangerous habits. Those were dark days; days I'm not proud of. Days when I couldn't even mother my children in a godly way. I ignored the consequences of my actions, which eventually produced a devastating pattern of behavior. But, hey, I'm a new mom . . . with new responsibilities . . . with excuse after excuse to care for my family in a comfortable way . . . so I deserve these treats, right? Oh, if you haven't noticed, there's a special shelf in our walk-in closets for all our excuses! A shelf I visited far too often.

Why is it when we look at temptation square in the face, we never think about what tomorrow holds? Do we ever consider the whole "choice vs. consequence" concept before we act? Aren't there times when we just choose to ignore what our gut tries to tell us? Yes, we do. And we pay the price.

My excuses soon turned into an attitude of entitlement. The truth was, I just didn't want to face up to the lie I could never change. Even when I followed the "diet rules" to the letter, there was no change. I was tired of fighting to constantly stick at my goal weight. Those weekly weigh-ins rose and plummeted, along with my heart rate and self-esteem. Every empty, unmet promise added more pain. My unrealistic expectations were not practical, thus I rode the emotional roller coaster over and over again. In the end, I had exhausted my hope of staying thin, healthy, or fit.

My self-worth was gone. At this point, giving up seemed like the least painful alternative. Instead of an introspective look at the real problem—me—I ignored all of my issues along with the hope of ever accomplishing my goal.

I wasn't worthy of forgiveness, and I certainly would never be free from the foodie prison which held me captive. After all the years of self-help methods gone wrong, I couldn't even help or love myself. So why would anyone else, outside my husband who married into this, want to love me? I had rejected myself right up to the measure of 244 pounds. I was on a slow descent and found myself on the first and closest exit ramp.

Dysfunction flowed through my veins like jet fuel to an airplane. Dr. Geraldine Downey, professor of psychology at Columbia University, so aptly described it: "Rejection (or dysfunction) knows no bounds, invading social, romantic and job situations alike. And it feels terrible because it communicates subliminal messages of unloved or unwanted, or not in some way valued." What a perfect description of my world at the time.

The Truth About Dysfunction

Dysfunction looks like tight fitting jeans and comes in all shapes and sizes. No matter the size, shape, or color, the bottom line of any dysfunction is: It hurts! It slashes your confidence, weakens a foundation of trust, casts a shadow of shame and guilt, and many times leaves its victim on the curb like a bag of garbage. Oh, that's not all…this powerful force tells us we're uninvited to a life of joy and happiness! Most of us, at one time or another, believe such words to be true.

Whoever said, "Sticks and stones can break my bones, but words will never hurt me," was a liar! Words hurt! If you have been on the receiving end of your fair share of negative words, then you don't need any more added to the mounds of dysfunctions you've already collected. In your private and personal misery, your emotions are wrapped up tight. Acceptance has been blocked, and you only hear a constant storm of painful thoughts. Mental anguish is a daily battlefield within your soul, which silently kills your worth and value.

Dysfunction of any kind unveils all types of darkness inside of us—some we didn't even know existed at the time. All my past wounds, guilt, and shame—raised their ugly heads and spewed lies, sabotaging my little to nonexistent self-esteem. I soon began to believe those lies and became my own worst critic. Those years propelled darkness to a whole different level.

We all have our stories of hurts, abuse, and childhood heartbreaks. Dysfunction leaves a person feeling less than worthy. When you feel shunned, the feeling wars against Jesus' blood-bought confidence in you. As you continue to dwell on a low self-image, your heart becomes hardened and full of skepticism concerning friendships, love, and trust.

Dysfunction creates distance, rather than intimacy with God. This mindset leads to the ultimate dysfunction: *Will you ever be acceptable to God?* Can He forgive you for what you have done? With a negative mindset, you're constantly

Dysfunction creates distance, rather than intimacy with God.

disappointed with yourself as you play the comparison game. The chants in your mind are amplified: *You're fat. No one likes you. You're too big to sit here. You go play over there with the fat kids. You're too slow to be in this game. You're so fat, that plaid you're wearing looks like a shower curtain. Why are you eating that cookie when you know it makes you fatter?*

Have you ever wanted a little breathing room for your self-esteem? Lord knows... *I have.* I was a prisoner in my own skin with a secret life tucked away in my closet. My "skinny" dream had consumed me for years. The failed attempts at losing weight only produced a false hope to even try again. That place of dysfunction—created only in my mind—consumed the whole me. I was victimized and literally paralyzed in my soul. Without even realizing it, I was impoverished—not financially, but emotionally.

Mother Teresa explained it like this: "We think sometimes that poverty is only being hungry, naked, and homeless. The poverty of being unwanted, unloved and uncared for is the greatest poverty. We must start in our own homes to remedy this kind of poverty." This was my story! That is, until 2006—the year my heart broke and I realized the truth: Janelle was Janelle's worst enemy.

Who Said That?

Terry and I attended a home fellowship group with my good friend Dana Craig and her husband Jeff. At this meeting, we all began to share our dreams and what we believed God was leading us to do. Terry shared his dream to be financially free so to travel the country and visit historical landmarks (He's always been our family historian). Then, it was my turn.

I sat on Dana's hunter green couch in the middle of her living room. All of a sudden, I blurted out, "I just want to be who God created me to be!" At last, it was out! All I wanted was to be ME! There was only one problem: I didn't know who "me" was.

As soon as I said those words, I turned around as to ask, "Who said that?" Yep, this was one of those moments when I knew something so out-of-the-blue had to come from someone else!

You see, at the time, I made a living with words. My husband says I could talk to a post from now until next week, no matter if it's listening or not! He's right. But when this life-changing statement popped out of my mouth, it did more than fill up the empty and awkward silence in the room. It was a hidden vision released that turned around my life's trajectory.

In a small moment, God started His big changes in me. I had long before relinquished my big dream of being skinny and resigned myself to the way I was: unchangeable. But in one sentence, one declaration, God planted a seed of desire in me to change.

Of course, I inwardly longed to be delivered and free, but I couldn't put my hope up for auction anymore. For me to be free from my past and to break the hold food had on my life was beyond my grasp—a sacrifice I was fearful to make. But, God had other plans!

He spoke truth into me, saying, "Janelle, you are the one holding yourself prisoner by your choices and own negative safety net. You are the one who has hindered My best for you, My child." I'll never forget the shock that rushed through my body. Suddenly, I knew I was entering a new life-changing season, and my destiny was forever set.

The Challenge

In 2007, I was the morning show co-host at The House FM Radio Station in Ponca City, OK. One day, my co-host and great friend, Brent McCoy, gave me a challenge: to be the captain of a contest sponsored by our station called "The Total Fitness Challenge." My heart reeled— not from excitement, mind you, but from fear!

I knew this would be a great challenge for our listeners, but I just couldn't see myself enduring another weight loss program, only to fail once again. Not only me, but I would lead our listeners—some who were very close friends of mine—down a path of failure, as well. I couldn't, wouldn't, and had no desire to publicly humiliate myself.

I went into this contest kicking and screaming. My on-air confident personality was not matched with a desire to change my weight, even though it was a big issue in my life. So, I decided to simply go through the motions of the contest. Because I had allowed fear to layer over my inner most, beautiful, fearfully and wonderfully made self for years, the thought of leading people to lose weight in a month's time was a daunting task. But, I forced myself to go with the crazy idea and set out to try again. Hey, it was only a month, right? It would soon be a distant memory. The worst that could happen was I would add another failure to my list.

But before I knew it, a small competitive spirit rose up within me to not only participate, but contribute to the real challenge that laid ahead. Of course, being at my all-time heaviest weight—244 pounds— probably had something to do with my change of attitude. Plus, I had my own troop of accountability looking to me to lead them.

As we entered the contest, Brent threw out another challenge to me: to encourage my team with some exercise goals. I didn't like the idea *or* him for suggesting it; moreover, I hated myself for even agreeing to participate. Again, I battled with myself. How could I lead listeners to lose weight and get fit? I was so messed up spiritually, physically, and emotionally with all my self-condemnation, that I couldn't see a way out of this pit for me, let alone others.

Let's Just Get This Over With

For the sake of my team and our show, I dug deep and even researched some verses God brought to my mind, which empowered me to believe this time could be the real deal. By all appearances, it looked like I was succeeding . . . and loving it. But the reality was, I was still faking it— still living under a disguise to gain attention and approval.

But by the end of the month-long contest, I had lost 15 pounds! With a little motivation, I decided to see how much more I could lose. Those 15 pounds kick-started my hope and whispered that I might not be a huge piece of chopped liver after all. With my many unsuccessful tries, my "loser" mentality was slowly disappearing.

Making It Real

So how cluttered is your closet? What emotional outfits have you worn? Do you need to toss those damaged feelings out? Stop and take an emotional inventory. Take a hard look at your past, your childhood, and all those memories that still tempt you to speak negatively about yourself. I have found when we carry our wounds and issues through life, our perception is off kilter. That's why it's so important to match your perspective with the truth of God's Word.

Think About It

You may not realize it right now, but whenever you ask the Father for direction and help, He bends down and listens to your cries. The Bible says He even counts and collects your tears. Confessing your inadequacies to the Father simply means that you can't do this journey on your own. And, He loves it when you are dependent on Him, especially when it's heart work. Once He starts to reveal His love towards you, on the inside of you, the healing process has been initiated. First, ask Him to help you find the source of your insecurities.

1. What are the reasons you run to food for comfort? Are you stressed? Exhausted? Is your work environment or home life filled with tension?

2. Instead of grabbing a stack of Oreos, talk to God to ease the stress or tension.

3. What is one habit you can change to take a step toward self-improvement?'

Kickstart Action Steps

Read Psalm 139. Focus on verses 23-24, where David asked God to search and know his heart. Allow God to bring a healing to your hurts and wounds, release you from your burdens, and change your behavior. This is your first step to freedom. If you feel unworthy to come to God, remember He wants you healed more than you do!

Prayer

Father, I am grateful for Your love and grace. Thank You for revelation and for how You illuminate my mindset for change. Help me to overcome the wounds within me and the profound roots of anxiety that have kept me in bondage. Help me to see You for who You truly are and not through my tainted glasses. Rid me of any wrong thoughts and enlighten my understanding of Your grace. Tear down the walls and barriers that have kept me from receiving Your healing for my hurts and hang-ups. Thank You, Father, for the healing in my heart. I receive Your healing by faith. Thank You for restoration and for transformation. Thank You for the dreams and plans for me. I trust You to do what only You can do. In Jesus' name. Amen.

Notes

Chapter 4

Cleaning Out Your Closet

Challenge accepted. Challenge met. Challenge conquered! Victory was mine! Well, for a minute anyways. Yes, the radio contest was over, but my new journey to discover the real me had just begun.

While inwardly rejoicing in my conquest (truthfully, I was just glad to finish the stupid thing), the outward results were not immediately noticeable. The enemy was still lurking around, feeding me lies, even seducing me with temptation to fall back in love with the tasty pleasures of life. Then, a new challenge . . . one I never dreamed I could accomplish.

A few weeks after the radio contest ended, I was sitting in church in the third row, third seat in. I'll never forget the place where things changed for me—I call it the seat of transformation. That particular Sunday, our pastor challenged the entire church to a three-day fast. Now, he wasn't talking your average, run-of-the-mill, miss-a-meal-a-day fast; oh no, he was serious! He included anything that was hindering your walk with the Lord like food, T.V., social media, and other activities. His intention was for us to discover what we loved more than God. Gulp!

I knew at that moment what God was doing. He was challenging me to a food fast so I could set my heart right before Him. But I wasn't in agreement . . . at all! The first thing I said to God was, "Wait, God, surely You don't want me to give up food for three whole days! Haven't I already given up enough of that already?" Then, God responded with a question for me: "Janelle, do you love Me more than food?" Gulp . . . harder! "I guess I do, God." And He told me, "Okay, then let's see."

By now, it was no surprise that food was a big stronghold in my life. My sin of gluttony was seriously sinister. My sweet tooth had deceived and trapped my wounded heart. So, I knew these three days would be hard . . . make that, miserable . . . no, make that unbearable!

As I sat in my "wilderness" seat, I was heavier spiritually than I can ever remember. I felt so hopeless and so alone. Then I did the only thing I knew to do: I cried out to Jesus, asking for the strength to do this. Thankfully, He heard my cry, and granted me just what I needed to survive: His amazing grace.

Time to Make a Change

Here's something that might be a shocker to you: *Great things happen when you put God first in your life!* Okay, maybe that's not an earth-shaking revelation, but how many times do we need to be reminded of this simple yet powerful truth? Here's even better news: *Jesus has defeated our emotions—the confessed ones and the unconfessed ones—taking their weight when He died on the cross of Calvary!* All the shame, guilt, rejection, and every other negative residue of sin is erased . . . for good! Knowing and believing this fact not only sets us free from patterns of wrong thinking, it also allows us to see our real identity—the person God created us to be.

It could be all the negative emotions from your past are blocking your true identification. Perhaps your excess weight issue is a result of an unresolved childhood emotion. All the memories of not being good enough, pretty enough, skinny enough, funny enough, and all the other inadequacies formed your shame list, which evolved into adult dysfunction. We all replay those negative childhood moments where we longed to hear, "I love you just the way you are," over the comparative statement of, "Why can't you be more like your sister?" Those childhood labels we keep are killer. Let's talk about labels a little more.

Do you realize many labels we bear oftentimes originate from our parent's inadequacies, imperfections, and failures? It's true. And, if we never take those labels to the cross and wash them with the blood of Jesus, they will continue to shape our lives until we don't even recognize ourselves. My life is a perfect example. Due to my parent's inability to show true, heart-felt love towards me, I spent a good part of my childhood and young adult life searching for approval, validation, self-worth, and significance.

I never knew what it was like to be really loved, not even at home. When I finally began to dig into those issues later in life, it uncovered a whole chuck wagon full of other emotions: anxiety, destruction, fear, guilt, shame, jealousy, false humility, discouragement, despair, anger, indecision, to name a few. I thought I was just looking for love, but the enemy was wreaking havoc on my weakness.

/>

One of the most debilitating emotions I had to deal with was shame. I was constantly ashamed of my weight, my looks, my laugh, my family, and my decisions. You name it, I've been ashamed of it somewhere along the road. What I found to be true is shame is the trap that keeps you in a personal prison, and guilt is your gatekeeper.

For years, I lived in a self-prison where my thoughts were dominated by my warped self-worth. My past left me broken-hearted, vulnerable, inadequate, and certainly embarrassed. Shame convinced me that if I—a good Christian woman and mother of two— told anyone I didn't have it all together, they would no longer like me. Fear convinced me that if I was ever exposed and found lacking, I would be rejected even more.

That was before my three-day journey.

Shame is the trap that keeps you in a personal prison, and guilt is your gatekeeper.

The Journey Begins

During my three days without food, God downloaded so much into my spirit. It's amazing what we hear when we're hungry—naturally and spiritually. While I've already shared a few things God said, what I'm about to say was the most important of them all. In fact, it could be the most important line you read in this book, especially if you are in need of a desperate change in your life. Are you ready? Taking ownership of my own issues was the beginning of my transformation.

Allow me to explain further. So much of my agony was birthed from my own anxieties. I had yielded to the most effective tool for temptation—food—which prolonged my bondage, my "wilderness journey" and kept me separated from God. As if all my mess wasn't enough, the enemy put a cherry of doubt on top, which severely hindered my willingness to break free from my emotional pit and black hole of depression. But, I had to push through all the layers if I were ever to be free.

After taking ownership of my life, my first move was to get honest with God, complete with all my negative emotions on my sleeve. When I say, "honest," I mean completely, brutally, naked honest! The first thing on my agenda—which was also the hardest—was coming to grips with my past.

Confronting my emotions was heart wrenching, but enabled me to be completely open and personal with God without any reservations. For the first time I can ever remember, I finally found myself at a point of total trust. And who better to trust my life to than the One who knows the deepest places of my heart!

My honest confessions before the Lord unveiled a startling truth: I had not invited Him into my weight loss journey. At that moment, I needed a big touch of grace and a whole lot of tissues! Never in my life had I felt such a physical weight lift off of my heart and shoulders. But through all those tears of confession, admission, and expression, God's healing touch of grace gave me two new labels: clean and unashamed!

When I finally submitted to God's whole forgiveness and grace, I discovered that my perspective of my earthly father had transferred to my image of my heavenly Father. This was my real first breakthrough to properly seeing God and myself. The opinion of my heavenly Father was warped by my own heart's deception.

Because my father never expressed real love to me, I automatically thought that God saw me the same way: unlovable, unworthy, and incapable of being loved by anyone—especially myself.

Author Brennan Manning puts it like this: "Grace is the active expression of His love. The Christian lives by grace as Abba's child, utterly rejecting the God who catches people by surprise in a moment of weakness—the God incapable of smiling at our awkward mistakes, the God who does not accept a seat at our human festivities, the God who says 'You will pay for that,' the God incapable of understanding that children will always get dirty and be forgetful, the God always snooping around after sinners." Such horrible lies I had swallowed regarding God's Pure Grace!

I'll never forget how God's voice made me feel: loved, accepted, treasured, and valued. Even now while writing this book, I'm weeping with tears of joy. My lifelong dream was just to be loved and accepted by my parents. In that solemn, holy moment, God asked me if

I was ready to discard the old unhealthy me and accept my new identity in Him. Was I ready for the new, healthy version of Janelle? Yes, I was!

When the Lord began speaking His words of life and love to my spirit, they not only healed my shattered heart but they let me see a much bigger picture. All those years I spent setting myself up for one diet failure after another was nothing more than a performance void of God's grace. Now, the truth was revealed. God was preparing me for my role on His divine stage. He had to bring me to the end of myself so the miracle could happen.

He had to bring me to the end of myself so the miracle could happen.

In the end, I made it through the three-day fast! It was one of the hardest things I've ever done, but one of the most rewarding. During those three *very long* days, God revealed some things to me, about me, that helped change my life. Here are a few:

❖ **I was deceived.**
Just like Eve in the Garden, my desires were misdirected, mostly to my number one source of comfort: food!

❖ **The root was exposed.**
The source of my constant need for approval, which I battled my entire life, was exposed. It was the void left in me from my earthly father. No matter what I tried or how much food I ate, nothing could ever fill the hole left in my heart.

❖ **I loved food too much.**
Wow, what a revelation! I was much more than a "foodie"—I was addicted to food. It was an idol in my life that I used as a coping mechanism instead of faith in Christ.

❖ **I didn't love God as much I thought.**
Ouch! Every Christian says that they love God, but my number one love was food. My heart really did long for Him, but I had

succumbed to the fear and approval of man instead of walking in my authority in Christ.

❖ **I needed an overhaul.**
It became painfully clear that my appearance, my image according to people's opinion, or my constant fear of man would never make me the person God designed me to be. God had to redesign my heart. I needed to put my heart, mind, and soul on the surgeon's table and let Him do the work.

Those three days were a wakeup call. My spiritual alarm clock went off and, thankfully, I answered! Changes had to be made. I had to return to my obedience to Him. He, once again, had to be my first priority in life. Everything else would fall into place.

My mind could not keep still. Thoughts raced like rockets. Could this really be happening? Could I really be loved by the Creator of the universe when I can't even love myself? Was there enough of His grace for me? Would I be able to really live for the first time in my life? It was like a dream . . . . . . But it was real.

Can't Fix Me!

On the same day, another stark revelation came to me. You can spend your entire life trying to constantly fix yourself, but when you come to the end of yourself, guess what? You're still messed up!

For years, I tried everything, in every way, and by all the right ways to lose weight. I ate the cabbage soup, cut out all bread and sweets for a season, cut back on the sodas, ate five little meals a day, learned to like raw tuna, and got a gym membership. I even adopted the alternating day "milk and banana" plan. In the end, the idols I allowed into my life only led me astray and lured me into their deceptive devices, one tasty morsel at a time. I was a walking zombie, secluded and seduced into a tailspin that God alone could rectify.

All I wanted was for God to fix me.

I was totally done trying to be a "good girl." That wasn't working. I was tired of always looking backwards. I was ready to move forward. My broken heart needed a reason to hope again. I needed something new, something I had never tried before... I needed Jesus to give me a new healthy heart in a real and practical way. So, I cried out with a few simple words and a lot of tears. And, He answered.

That day—sitting on that third row, in the third seat—God reached down and saved me…again. He heard my prayer. He answered my heart's cry. He heard my true self crying out in my final desperation, and my life was forever changed. Oh, if you're wondering why all the references to where I was sitting, it's simple: When you have a life-altering encounter, you remember the details!

I shudder to think what could have happened if God hadn't rescued me. My own doings only produced more misery. Many days I questioned what else life had to offer. Was this all there was to living as a Christian wife and mom? Was I going to train my children to overeat and overindulge? What legacy was I going to leave? Was this all that God had for me? Perhaps you've experienced this kind of darkness— the darkness that creeps into your thoughts, leading you to believe there is only one solution to relieve this depth of mental and emotional pain. If so, know this: There is hope and there is an answer!

Divine Intersections

There comes a point in your life when you choose to try again. A time when you must decide to let hope have another chance to do its work in your life. But, these decisions do not come without a price tag. To find God's amazing love—the only love worth searching for—will require self-sacrifice. You must give up something you love (i.e. food) for something you love *more*. It's a model set in motion by God Himself.

God loved His Son, Jesus, but He sacrificed Him for all mankind. Jesus loved His life, but He willingly gave it up for something He loved more—you! I knew I had to give up something; I just didn't know what at this point.

Whole surrender to God requires a holy exchange. I can't adequately describe the process, except to say in those moments of complete and full confession, you become a beautiful being before your heavenly Father. It's His strong gentle voice that breaks down

I chose grace instead of trying to save face…

the heart barrier and shows His love and mercy once again. Gone are the labels from your past, your parents, those created by negative thought patterns, your own shame list, and the guilt which captivates your self-esteem and identity.

There's such a joy in repentance. Repentance is more than an emotion, it's changing the way you think and what patterns your behavioral responses.

During those three teary, grueling days of fasting, I experienced a giant collision of confession, repentance, and commitment. I had to strap in for some very rough and tough admissions. My will and heart *had to be* surrendered to Him. All of my efforts to clean up my act had failed. I needed Jesus to save me again in a new way: from myself!

It was at this intersection that God broke a big stronghold of food in my life and began His glorious story of hope written on my open heart.

I embraced my imperfections and confessed my obsessions; I gained the strength to change as my heart softened to God's truth. In one moment, I literally stepped from my bondage of gluttonous sins into the freedom that awaited me. Despair gave way to hope and weakness was replaced by a supernatural strength.

My earnest desires changed from the inside out. No more running to food for comfort. Peanut M & M's were no longer my sweet savior. Ice cream would never be a healing salve for my hurting heart ever again. Upon confession of my obsessions, God responded by gently cupping my chin and saying, "Come to me my little broken vessel. I will give you rest."

That day, I made the best exchange: I chose grace instead of trying to save face any longer. It was one of the hardest decisions I've ever made, but through that exchange I am now truly a new creation in Christ! The old has gone; the new has come.

My closet got cleaned!!

Your Life, Your Freedom

This was my story. Now how about you? Are you ready to let God change you from the inside out? Are you willing to *undo* your will so that God can *redo* His new thing in you? Do you need freedom that comes from coming clean before God? There's no guilt or shame there. Once you come to Him with everything, grace erases your past. Jesus paid the price for you on the cross so that you could see yourself rescued, redeemed, and valuable.

Trusting God is the first step in your faith. But, it also takes faith to believe that even though you are who you are, and done what you've done, you're still able to overcome strongholds, struggles, and your past through Christ. Whatever the issue, the emotion, or the cause of your personal landslide, there is only one freedom at the end of it all. His name is Jesus. If you are tired of the weight of your own burdens, then something has to change. A decision has to be made.

You can continue to carry your personal baggage with you, or surrender it to the One who loves you more than you can ever imagine. It's your choice. Before any process of positive change can begin, there must be some ground work established along with safe, healthy boundaries. The first is realizing the root of all your issues, habits, and hang-ups, and addictions is the same: the deception of sin. Confessing this to God is a requirement for Him to activate His holy healing in your life.

The world can't meet your validation needs like our heavenly Father's approval, acceptance, and stamp of love can. The enemy will always twist the truth. The lie that you can never be free of bondage is a ploy that Satan uses often. He doesn't care how he isolates you, he wants you constantly defeated by your own baggage. But the truth is, as a child of God, YOU are worth saving! The work of Jesus Christ on the cross nailed down your identity on a hill far away called Calvary! And because of this truth—you have victory, too!

Welcome to your new label: ***forgiven and free!*** If Jesus sets you free, you are truly free! This is where your baggage becomes luggage. Your self-will tries to make you think you're not strong enough to let go. That's a victim mentality. Get rid of it! Renew your mind through God's Word. Just as it took many years for you to fit into false labels, it will take time for the new you to be your natural instinct. Hang in there. It does become easier as you daily confess your need to be changed. It's time to clean out that closet . . . and never go back!

Making It Real

What personal issues have weighed you down? Do you have a past you can't undo? These sorts of things can distort your thinking into negative emotions of guilt, shame, and condemnation. But God's unconditional, non-judgmental grace changes everything! Will you take time to receive a little grace today? Your life will never be the same.

Think About It

1. What needs to change to get you back on the right path of health?

2. Are you ready to humbly surrender to accept you can't fix yourself outside of help by the Holy Spirit?

3. If you saw yourself the way God sees you, would you be able to love yourself, just like you are?

Kickstart Action Steps

Read 2 Corinthians 5:17. God has gone to great lengths and sacrifice to re-label you. Even Bible "greats" like Paul and David were re-labeled. Search God's Word to help clear any labels from your past. Accept the truth about His deep love for you. Praise Him for His complete love towards you, even when you have labeled yourself unlovable.

Prayer

God, I look to You. I want to see You and know You. I want to see myself reflected from Your eyes of love. You know me from the inside out, and You love me anyway. Forgive me for believing the labels of my past that contradict what Your Word says I am. I am whole in You.

I thank You that, in You, I live and move and have my being. Thank You for changing the way I think. Because of Jesus' sacrifice, I have new life. I find worth, today, in His shed blood on the cross. I receive

Your grace and mercy today. Thank You for re-writing my name, revealing my purpose, and restoring my covenant with You. I'm not looking back, but moving forward towards the heavenly goal You have set for me. In Jesus's name. Amen.

Notes

Chapter 5
The Most Awesome Outfit You Will Ever Wear

"Phew! It's dark, dusty, and a bit suffocating in here." That was my reaction when I truly saw my closet for the first time after my three days with God. Something about the darkness made my bones shudder. Once my closet was clean, I finally could see all the skeletons which had previously hung silent. They were everywhere—hanging, laying on shelves, and tucked in the very back corners. Dare I say that's a place we all want to avoid?

It's amazing how many people cling to their past failures like a badge of honor. That's exactly what I did for years. Deep down, those failures in dropping pounds severely limited my life, but I thought somehow, some way, I could fix myself all by my lonesome. Little did I realize that I couldn't. I needed the power of the Holy Spirit, and as much as I needed Him to help, I was far, far from His power.

Let's face it. Cleaning out your closet isn't easy—even *with* the help of the Holy Spirit. There are some corners you just don't want to look at. Pent up emotions, from years of self-abuse, make you afraid to even crack the door. I get that. Fear of man's opinions held me hostage for so long, I didn't want to come clean before anyone . . . especially God. I mean, how could He really love someone like me? How could He show any grace to a multi-offender such as me? How could He take me back, especially now at my heaviest weight ever? Even if I were to cast out all of my bad outfits, would I be fit to wear His righteous garments? I was a hard sell on God's grace. We all are at one time or another in a mindset that convinces ourselves that we are unworthy.

Wearing an Original

Funny how those pesky skeletons in our closets stay hidden until it's time to make room for some new outfits. Then, they start to clatter. Maybe it's time to tackle yours. If you're uncomfortable looking at your own list of errors or closet full of skeletons, that's okay. I'll go first and let you take a closer look at mine.

I was so thankful that God, by His Spirit, swept my closet clean. I was free and forgiven, but there was a problem: I didn't live free. The enormity of my sin blanketed my shoulders like a wounded soldier. Even though free on the inside, I still walked around in prisoner clothes, bound by hidden chains. I had to come to grips with the whole of me and make some hard decisions concerning what I allowed into my life. The things that were toxic and not enriching my soul—mainly my food idol—had to go.

Food was on the throne of my heart, the place God should have been seated. It was there to stay until I removed my love for it and let it fall away. It was a hard fall! But the deeper issue was the sacrifice in my heart—a resetting to receive a more complete love than I could ever imagine or describe.

Without question, I have lost a large amount of weight and a ton of spiritual baggage. But it hasn't been easy. I, too, have ridden the roller coaster of emotions on this journey. Not only did I lose 104 pounds the first time around, I backslid to gain 30 pounds back. While enjoying my lightest weight, I let go of what I knew worked and started to walk in my own strength. Then, I don't really know what happened. A series of events kicked me in the gut, causing me to lose sight of ever becoming fit, trim, and brimming with hope. But instead of handing it to me on a silver platter laced with chocolate gauche, God took me down a road that tattooed grace on my heart.

This is what I found: no matter how far out of reach we might feel, God's grace and forgiveness is ever further reaching! It knows no boundaries or depths. Not only does God find the skeletons and awkward fitting outfits you've tried to wear, His grace replaces them with new robes of righteousness. The world and all its opinions can never hold a candle to the love and grace God has for us, no matter how many past skeletons we have. God's grace is matchless, unrelenting, undeserved, merciful, and mighty to save us from the pain we have caused ourselves.

Have you ever watched the Oscar's or Emmy Awards and dreamed of wearing one of those gorgeous original designs? I know I have! Well, you and I might not ever be on the red carpet in an original Armani or Ralph Lauren, but we have a greater unique outfit to wear: God's grace!

God's grace isn't some knock-off or cheap imitation. It's the outfit for all seasons, it fits all sizes, and it lasts forever! Not only that, but when you wear His grace, you can throw away all those scratchy, itchy, irritating labels, plus those misfit outfits you've been trying to get into. God's grace is a style like none other. When you wear it, you will shine from ear to ear, head to toe, finger-tip to finger-tip, and from the inside out!

It's never too late to start or to start over! If you've never worn God's gorgeous, awesome gown of grace, you can begin today. It might feel as though God has left you all alone in your misery of Cheetos and ice cream sundaes. And where was He when those 40 pounds snuck up on your back side as you fought through a horrible medical crisis? I can tell you where He was: right beside you the entire time. He was with you then and He is with you now. He wants to swallow your loneliness! And He loves you more than you could ever fathom.

It's Getting Real, Now!

I hope that you're shouting, dancing, and thanking God for His love and grace, but let me give you a challenge! That's right, a good ol' in-your-face challenge—along with some hope at the same time. Are you ready? Here it is: **You need to stop looking to food for your comfort and significance in this world.**

Ouch! Time to speak the truth. No matter how long you look or how much grace you experience, your food addiction will never produce the comfort you need or the significance you crave. True self-significance and comfort only come from one source: the comforter Himself—the Holy Spirit.

This isn't a charge of condemnation, but encouragement. Lord knows it took me long enough to finally see that He was my answer to everything, including my health. As a Christian, I knew God cared about my spiritual walk, but I didn't consider He cared about it all. The truth is, He loves us through and through—spirit, soul, and body. Our emotional needs are on His heart. Our mental needs are on His mind. Our physical needs are on His daily planner. Our spiritual needs are His deep concern. The bottom line is this: **God is more concerned about our wholeness than our happiness!**

.But, isn't that what we're looking for? A deep inward satisfaction that the world so artistically artificially offers? Aren't we all looking for our place to belong?

God is more concerned about our wholeness than our happiness!

If that is your desire, then let God begin writing your new story—one of restoration and hope. That's been my testimony for the last 10 years. God miraculously took me from a place of hopelessness to one of hope-filled restoration. And, it can be your story, as well. Believe me. It's true. There is hope for you just like there was and still remains for all of us.

Okay, here's challenge number two: ***Stop excusing your weight as, "God wants me this way!"*** No, He doesn't! Yes, He loves you in that condition, but He doesn't want you to stay there.

Which label of dieter are you? Life-timer? Professional? Worn thin? The "I've tried everything" dieter? Or are you just wondering where God is in all your accumulated list of failures? Here's something that might shock you: The grace of God cannot be earned by your best, clean, or consistent eating habits. It's a gift. Each time you go to God, He is faithful to forgive. He's not judging, blaming, accusing, or holding out on you. He simply loves you because He *is* love.

And He's waiting to share that love with you, just like He did me. No matter how many times you mess this up or run away from Him, He is always waiting with arms open wide to take you back into His love.

My "Awesome"

Imagine that we are having coffee together right now, and I gently clutch your stretched-thin heart. Now, I'm three inches from your face and I say, "God wants you to be brave. He has better for you." (Excuse my coffee breath!) Don't we all want to live a better life? Of course, so stick with me. I have more freedom to share with you. Then choose to get to know "Awesome." That's right . . . "Awesome" . . . Awesome God!

All my life I had been looking for someone faithful and true, but never found it . . . that was until one Good Friday at a church in Kingfisher, Oklahoma.

My soul was so stark and empty. For months I questioned, "God, where are you?" Then on Good Friday 1988, as a young mom sitting alone on a cold pew, God invited me into His grace, acceptance, and wholeness. It was my *best* Friday! On that day, God's holy love settled deep within this young mom's broken heart once and for all. It was the day I realized that Awesome wanted to know me in an intimate, jealous way.

That day, I accepted Jesus Christ as my Lord and Savior for real. No longer was I hanging onto my parent's faith. This was the day that an *awesome God found me*! With my little family clamoring at my feet, God became the center of my life. From the moment I invited Jesus into my heart, everything changed. Friend, the Gospel changes everything! Awesome knew my time was ripe for surrender—and surrender I did. He delighted in me. Wow, imagine that . . . someone delighting in you! Just imagine.

Psalms 149:4 is one of my favorite verses in the Bible. It says: "For the Lord takes pleasure in His people; He will beautify the humble with salvation." (NKJV)

How reassuring to know that a Holy God delights in each one of us, regardless of our past or the sum total of our sins. The word "delight" has such a wonderful connotation. It means "to savor." Wine tasters know this term very well. In the process of finding the best wine, the art of savoring is part of their considerations in their selection. They take a sip, roll it around their tongue, finding delight in each sensation. And when they taste the right one, they can appreciate everything about it.

I didn't realize it at the time, but Awesome had been whispering love into my soul for a while as I cried myself to sleep many nights when I didn't hear, "Good-night, I love you" from the other room. My

How reassuring to know that a Holy God delights in each one of us, regardless of our past or the sum total of our sins.

tear-stained pillow memories stick with me sometimes to this day, but God is healing that, too. That kind of missing love runs so deep.

In that emptiness and fractured state of what seemed like disrepair, He found me! I still can't understand it all, but I am so thankful for it. I'm so deeply grateful that Awesome saw me when my soul was so empty, and He didn't write me off or ignore me. He thought I was worth everything. I'm so thankful He delights in me and thinks I am something to embrace. Awesome found me, brought me to this place of grace, and knows everything about me.

And guess what? Awesome God wants to meet you, too.

The Gift

If you're still looking for your identity and place in this world, you will only find it in one place: Jesus! If you feel like your life doesn't matter, know that your matters, matter to God. You have to invite His sweet salvation voice into your heart and receive His gift of grace that flows from the cross. Ephesians 2:8-9 states: "For by grace you have been saved through faith, and that not of yourselves; it is the gift of God, not of works, lest anyone should boast." (NKJV)

In Ephesians Chapter 2, *The Message* version of the *Bible* describes this saving grace as "immense in mercy and with an incredible love, he embraced us." The New Living Translation terms God's grace as a "gift," nothing we can take credit for (Ephesians 2:8). And rightly so. While a gift to us who believe, grace comes at a great expense. It was costly and lasts our lifetime.

To make this personal, put your name in place of grace. For me, it reads, "For Janelle you have been saved, through faith." How awesome is that? God has carved **your** name on the cross by the blood of Jesus that heals and sets you free! God's amazing love and grace is waiting on you to simply believe. Maybe you've never surrendered your life to Jesus. The question is, what are you waiting for? Do you know that a Holy God is calling you? Jesus is calling to your heart one whispered grace note at a time. He is not going to reject you nor say you are not good enough.

Let Jesus draw and call you into His closeness. Let his gentle love fall on your heart today. How does this happen? It's easy. Take a minute to pray this prayer from your heart.

Dear God, I have sinned and ran from You. I want to know You as my Lord and Savior. I want to know Your love that doesn't measure and is enough to clean every one of my wrongs. Jesus, I ask You to come into my heart. I accept Your work as the payment for all my wrongs. Today, I say yes and surrender my heart to You. God, I accept your free gift of grace and the blood of Christ for my life. Thank You, Jesus, that You have paid the price for my life with Your work on the cross. Thank You for carving my name next to yours. Thank You, God, that You delight in me and may I now find my whole delight in You. I want to live for You, and I want the life of freedom that You have for me. Teach me how to live free in YOU alone. In Jesus' name. Amen.

If you prayed this prayer and meant it in your heart, you are now a believer in Jesus Christ! If you prayed this prayer and were already a believer, count this as a re-devotion of your heart's intent to put your sin and your past behind and start over.

Right now, you've been changed by the *saving grace* of Jesus Christ! You are forgiven and grace-embraced—forever. Signed, sealed, and delivered to Heaven's door. When you take your last gasp of breath on this earth, you will spend an eternity in Heaven with the One who just saved you. But, that's only one part of the story. You're not only saved by grace, grace also empowers you to find and live your calling on this earth.

The Assignment

When I gave my life to Jesus, I lost myself, yet found myself at the same time. Today, my identity completely rests in One who bled and died for me and not in who my parents said I wasn't. My name is carved in the wooden tree of grace! The "unwanted" label previously attached to my life now reads "loved," just as I am.

In the same year of my saving grace and new identity, God also clearly revealed my assignment on this earth. And it happened at the most unusual place.

Not long after giving my life to Jesus, I was driving down Main Street in Kingfisher with my two abundantly full-of-life children. As most young kids, they were enjoying the day bouncing in the back seat. Right in the middle of the day, and in the middle of my drive, God spoke to my heart and said, "They are only yours for a little while." At that moment, I thought He was only referring to my children, but some years later, I began to see the big picture.

That day, God was preparing me for two things: His supernatural claim of my two lovelies and my spiritual calling. Along with my natural family, God was saying, "I've called you to be a 'mother' to many. I've called you to mentor many moms and children who are trapped, trying to measure up to culture's imperfect standards." The rest is history.

How thankful I am that God looked beyond all of my faults, hurts, inadequacies, hang ups, and screw ups. He anointed me to speak life into the lives of women who, like me, grew up in a family with absentee love. Women who have dealt with the overwhelming thoughts of abandonment from when they were little girls. Women who have believed the lies of this world and have a skewed view of a holy God. That's my calling.
Now, how about yours?

Oh yes, you have a supernatural assignment just like me and every other person on the earth. Of all the billions and billions of people who have filtered through this planet, no one has ever been exactly like you. Not one. Even though you might not see it right now, God has put His eternal imprint on your heart—His stamp of approval for your purpose in life. He can see your divine potential through His infinite wisdom.

You have been made in His love image. To think of that kind of love is baffling—something you and I can never wrap our minds around.

Wear It Well

The faithful and true God has called and you have said, "Yes!" Now what? You have the opportunity to live out the rest of your life as the person God designed you to be. How do you enjoy what Awesome has for you? It starts by emptying yourself.

The emptier you are, the more God will fill you with beauty and brilliance. No one has ever had your exact set of experiences, thoughts, successes, or failures. No one thinks exactly like you. When you feel

like it's all been done before, and you will, the Holy Spirit whispers these words into your ear: "I want more of you."
That's it.

God wants more of you. Stop selling out to the things of this world. You don't wear *that* outfit well. There is one thing that this world can never offer you: your true identity in Christ. This culture lures your desires and leaves you lacking, but He who knows you by name will speak to your heart. He will shut out the world around you and bring you into a close relationship with Him.

Every day, God will gently lead you to win. His wholeness is made strong in your weaknesses. It's His strength that will get you through the next meal, the next bite, the next storm, the next anything! Along the way, take encouragement from His Word. God has given you another golden thread of hope to cling to. His grace is the most awesome outfit you will ever wear. Wear it well!

Making It Real

God's love and grace are enormous and everlasting, relentless and all-pursuing, all-consuming and all-covering. It's perfect in every area you lack. His love is calling you to rid yourself of toxic habits, outfits, and attitudes. Isn't it time for you to admit you need God's help? Perhaps you've done that. Have you fallen down again and again as you try to stand in your own strength?

There, and only there, will you find forgiveness of your past sins and a removal of those memories which have caused you years of heartache. Never forget the power of forgiveness. Release your past, and let God start your brand-new day, today.

Think About It

This step forward is so important in the whole scheme of who you are and are meant to be in this life. Your best defense in growing into your destiny is the distance placed between yourself and the giants that taunt you. So once again, let's clean out that closet and keep moving forward!

1. What "closet" or "cabinet" do you need to bravely open and do some serious clean up?

2. What can you do to separate yourself from the accuser and his lies?

3. What's one thing you can do, today, to help steamroll this change and move forward?

Kickstart Action Steps

When David confronted Goliath, he picked up five stones. This was not by accident as all throughout the Bible, the number five represents the grace of God. David only needed one. But what really killed Goliath was his blindness. The Bible says that you have a sword—the Word of God.

God's Word will "kill" your enemy every single time. Once you discover your true identity in Christ by the Word of God, you will be equipped with all the weapons you need to take back what the enemy has stolen. You will see the difference, I promise you. The battle is the Lord's. And you are worth the fight! His grace is sufficient for every battle.

This action step exercise is a bit different than the others. Find one verse that brings strength to your life. Write the truth of God's word down. Then write the verse on colorful post-it cards, scraps, napkins, whatever you have available. Don't delay this step. The longer you agree with what your enemy says against you, the harder it is to regain your confidence and courage. (And *remember to journal!*)

Prayer

Dear God, I confess that I can't do this on my own. I need You every step of the way. Help me to look to You for all things and not neglect my confession of them to You. I now understand how You like to hear my voice, too. Open my mind and heart to walk deeper with You in each area where I need you. Help me to remember the importance of your Word, the power of prayer, and the release in praise. I love You and thank You for being my deliverer, my savior, and my healer. In Jesus' name. Amen.

Notes

Chapter 6
A Hope That Fits You

$\mathcal{I}$ have lost over 100 pounds and have maintained half of my starting weight for years now. With the help of the Holy Spirit, I practice success through hard work, exercise, and faithful obedience to God's word every day. I have a choice to put God first in my life, seek His kingdom and righteousness—or go my own way. It's your choice, too.

Hope needs to start somewhere. And it's better when you take a look at what you need to change first and ask God how to best implement a good workable plan for you. All I know is that I was in a desperate place, what felt like the backside of a deserted place, and I needed a rescue. Does that sound like your story?

I had to come to Him with all my hurts, pains, issues, and—here's the key—an open heart ready to receive His solutions. Only *then* could He start the healing process. How often do we approach God with our long laundry list of troubles, complaints, and tribulations, only to miss the healing opportunities God has for us through our problems? We tend to be crippled by our negative perspectives, paralyzed by insecurities, and limited by the inability to gain momentum in any kind of plan. Therefore, our hope for progress is dashed.

Steven Furtick, lead pastor of Elevation Church in North Carolina, said it best: "Lots of times, our main problem isn't our problem. Our biggest problem is our perspective on our problem."

Very often we want our situation to change, when God desires to change us with our situation. The first step to find a hope that fits is to get to the root issue; because your food addiction is likely only the manifestation of deeper concerns. **I don't need to know where you have been to see where you are headed.**

When you get to the root issue of the sin inside of you and repent of that sin, you not only gain a fresh perspective of the problem, but of God's marvelous solution and plan for your life.

No, I don't know your health problems.

No, I don't know your personal issues.

No, I don't know the lies you have swallowed.

No, I don't know you. But I do know that God knows you inside and out. And He knows best how to help you. If your heart is broken, and you didn't plan to live life this way—with all the heavy chains dragging behind you—then read on.

Shedding Layers of Disappointment

You were supposed to be a singer, a dancer, or a candlestick maker. You wanted to be a mom, and life said you can't bear children. Your spouse was supposed to stick with you through thick and thin, but he didn't. You were supposed to send your son off to war to fight for freedom; instead he died to save it. You weren't supposed to bury your child. You never should have to carry an unborn baby to term and find out you're unable to hold life.

Oh yeah, one more thing.… that parent or friend you trusted shouldn't have treated you like a piece of trash. Or worse yet, you don't deserve the self-harm you have dished out upon yourself. You can't change your past, yet you can continue to let it haunt and hurt you. You can't change your accuser's voice in the back of your mind, endlessly taunting you about those regrets. You can't change without cleaning out your entire perspective.
How do I know? I've been there.

Have you been hurt by circumstances that have hit you hard and have left your heart dangling, damaged by thread-thin emotions and twisted ways of thinking? I know…I have, too. You can't get stuck in that place in your past, though. The wounds, bruises, cuts, and scrapes have been met with the harshness of life, and the totality of them has some deep imprints upon your heart. These cumulative negatives take a real toll on the mind.

Hope can't exist in these conditions. The breath of hope is suffocated by the wall of overwhelming pain closing around your heart. The heart is the wellspring of life and fed by our brain to either liberate or segregate. It's a small muscle, but it has a deep capacity to intrinsically connect to the brain with our God-given identity. The chambers within it can emotionally bind us captive in lies, sentencing us into our own personal prisons. Or it can liberate us with a hope that cultivates freedom.

There was a time when I desperately cried out for a freedom that I couldn't even touch because I didn't believe I deserved it. (Is that a tear I see in your eye, too?)

There *is* freedom waiting for you. All you have to do is ask God; seek Him for answers, and let His ways change you. Do you want to walk in the freedom God has for you but don't know where to start? Perhaps you've had all kinds of ideas of what should happen next or how the plan should look. Well, this next revelation is simple, but mind blowing. You'll want to underline it or copy it into your journal: **It doesn't matter what you think at all—what matters is what your Heavenly Father sees IN you and what He says ABOUT you.**

Once I came to that realization, I made a list of who I was and who I wasn't, then compared it with His truth. I was surprised to see the difference. I was caught in a web of lies only my Savior could get me out of. The end result was worth it.

Note to Self

Do you remember what it was like to be 12, with those awkward school photos and ill-fitting jeans? Do you hear those insecurities screaming at you right now? I know …. I know! I promise you this has a great healing purpose. When I set out to tell my story, I found a letter I wrote to myself when I was still very heavy. Like the saying goes, "If I had known then what I know now…." and believed there was hope back in *those* years—it would have changed my destiny. (Not to mention I wouldn't have been so….so…. well…12!)

I wanted to share my letter in its entirety. Please bear with me; this is raw and straight from the pages of my personal journal.

Dear younger me,
This is a terrible story. You're 12. You have zits on your nose, split ends, and you wear t-shirts that say things like "Go against the flow" with a little Christian fish swimming on them. You are a "plain" young lady, busting all the wrong seams in life…in those annoying awkward years you wish could pass you by.

You don't have a boyfriend, but you dream of him being one of the singers that croon a nightly love serenade from your record player. The guy you've been kissing secretly for years. Your best friend in the whole world knows it and has been feeding you lies that he likes you back. The reality is there's no way he even knows you exist. And you wouldn't like him anyway; he's fake and an imposter. Run away from that kind of love.

You are a mess. But you dream. You dream of living a content life behind a little white picket fence, driving a blue scooter to work, raising your 2.5 children in your perfect churchy pew. You dream of being entirely loved like that and swept away to a perfect beachy landscape every year. Keep on dreaming, girl! The perfect guy is being fashioned for you, who will be made to love you like you are—in your imperfections. Keep on dreaming because a TRUE love really does exist.

I see you and your little group of girlfriends who know how to giggle until late into the night. You eat cookie dough right out of the package and add extra butter to your macaroni and cheese because you don't care, yet, about what it will do to your thighs. I know your heart cries. I know what you are looking for, and you won't find it in the food or the friends you are looking at.

If I could take you out for coffee or a nice foamy vanilla latte (well, maybe ice cream–you won't start drinking coffee for many more years), there are some things I'd say to you. I would love to gently put my arm around you and tell you a few things to help you along this journey to find love. I want you to know these things now, so you can see it sooner rather than later. And while we are sitting face to face, please stop beating yourself up. You really don't know yourself yet.

If I could tell you one thing, it would be: You are loved. Love needs to be said. This world we live in searches so hard, wonders so long, and meanders around aimlessly, for the sake of finding love. You long for answers, but try to find them in the wrong places. And you settle for less than what true love represents.

You know those songs of sadness you sing to yourself? The ones that repeat verses of hate and regret over and over, like an anvil to your heart, and weigh heavy on your soul? You are on like the one millionth version of that same old song, singing deadly dirges to your heart and killing your self-esteem slowly and yet so softly. That's the only so-called love song you sing to yourself, but your throat chokes with hatred each time it repeats. So, you just continue to grow cold and silent to the voice, and let your plastered-on smile cover it all. I've seen you in your room crying on your bed. I've seen you go unheard. Don't give up on hope. Something tells me that if you knew it didn't have to be this way, you would have hope and see the love around you. I wish there was a shortcut to hope. I wish there wasn't such a distance from where you are now and *the place you long to be. I wish you would tell someone how you feel inside; you would not be so hard towards love later.*

Let me tell you what I have discovered about love and uncovered about you. First of all, it doesn't matter that you're not popular. I know you stare longingly at the cool kids' table in the cafeteria or those that are old enough to go off campus to the cool spot you are never invited to. I know you've heard a snicker or two when you walk by certain groups in the halls. They whisper about you and the way you are dressed, in homemade clothes that look like tents, loud prints, and those wide shoes that look like barges on those extra wide feet. Gee whiz, someone leaked the Intel that your foot is fat too. I know how you stand in front of the mirror and tilt your head from one side to the other, hoping the reflection improves day by day. But it never does.

I know you feel rejected by their snickers and jeers. Those jokes about being the capital of Maine? That was thanks to a teacher who pokes fun at you. A person who nicknamed you out of his need to be funny to the class. You want to hurt him bad. And how about that principal in the 3rd grade that boomed your track meet weight to the entire 3rd and 4th grade?

*No, he didn't even need a microphone; his voice covered the entire school. Everyone heard "103 pounds" proclaimed. And I saw that your heart silently ripped in shame that day. I've seen your silent cries for attention when you hang out with the girl in your grade that has the longest, blondest hair in school—the one born to be popular. I've seen your suffering. That homemade plaid skirt speaks volumes about how you feel about yourself. It's plain to see from here the sadness from the inside stuff screaming to get out. **I know how you feel, but you are going to be alright someday.***

*By not being popular you're actually learning some pretty important things: how to love all kinds of people, how to have a tender heart for those on the outskirts, how to dream and explore instead of conform and confine. Your creativity is growing, although you can't see it yet, and you're not cool enough to want to crush it. Your older self will thank you now for not fitting in. The mold you are trying to squeeze yourself into will be harder to break open once you get out of the confines of peer pressure. **Thank you for hanging in there and getting into that plaid dress.***

I even want to thank you for those corduroy jumpers, too. I thank you, my little friend, because I see you suffering in your cocoon of self-pity. Know this with a little seed of hope that you are going to be okay. You are going to be MORE than okay; you are going to be more than awesome. You are going to be free one day.

It's true about butterflies: There's beauty inside. If nothing ever changed, there'd be no butterflies. And just when you think it's over, it's not. So don't lose hope because you never know what tomorrow will bring. Just when a caterpillar thinks its life is over, it becomes beautiful. When you feel that you're about to fail, it might actually be that you're about to fly.

No one can do it for you—you must choose to use your wings. Your life is similar to that of a butterfly. You will go through many changes before you become something beautiful. There's a hope that is rising from the inside of you. Keep searching for it, and don't stop until you find it. Never underestimate the power that lies within you. It's always been there, too. You have to want it. You must desire to fly and be willing to give up being perfect. Butterflies can't see their wings. They can't see how beautiful they are, but everyone else can. You are a cocooned kind of beautiful.

I see you like God does. Right now, you can't see the transformation that is destined for you. Right now, all you can see is pain, and it's loud. Please don't give up. You can do it, little one, and freedom is on the other side. Don't settle for being a caterpillar when you have butterfly potential. Allow God to transform you from the inside out. The struggle you're in today is developing the strength you need for tomorrow. Don't give up. After every storm comes clear, open skies. Don't give up. Don't be afraid to grow. I've never seen a butterfly crawl back into its cocoon and become a caterpillar. Don't give up. Don't be so hard on yourself. Don't give up. I can't stress it enough. Don't give up.

You are becoming, and there's such delight and beauty in the process of change. I want you to know that you don't have to try so hard. We like you. We love you actually. And who is the "we?" God, your parents, your family, your friends. Those who you are afraid to be real with. Guess what, most of them don't like themselves either. In fact, they are so insecure they would rather pick on you so they don't have to think about their own changes.

I know you want to get it right—the grades, the youth group, and the heart-to-heart girl conversations by the lockers. And when you don't, you're really tough on yourself. You are your own worst critic. Slow down a little please. Girl, take a breath and just stop being the negative you. Take a deep breath of grace. You haven't quite figured this out yet...you're human. You are 12 going on 24. You are going to mess up a lot. You are a mess in progress; you are imperfect; you will be clumsy with words and hearts. BUT it's going to be okay. People want the real you, not the perfect good girl you think you have to be.

You're going to grow up, and the years will fly by. You'll trade your bike for a car. Your t-shirts for TJ Maxx tops. Your diary entries about boys, for a real live husband. It will be good and hard and beautiful and like nothing and everything you imagined. And you are well on your way to writing a beautiful story of freedom. You are a writer, with just enough funny to bust at times. **But you will learn to love people as you haven't been loved.**

My little friend, you will learn encouragement in the sad times, in the times of rejection, in the times of being lonely, in the dark parts. But you will also learn freedom in your heart parts. You are going to be better than just okay. You are going to be great! You have time to get there. Savor the moments. Hold on to today. Don't wish away the now for the not yet. Worry less. Laugh more. Love better. Speak Life. Stay up late while you can. Eat marshmallows more. Embrace grace and the Giver of it. Dare to be the brave heart that God has created you to be. Dare to love yourself. You're going to turn out just fine.
Love, Me

…..Anyone need a tissue?

When I was at my lowest point as a child, I wish I would have known what this letter held for me. At the loneliest place in my mind, I needed some hope. Physically, I was ready to put my pleasure needs aside to get to my goal. Emotionally, I needed forgiven for how I tried over and over to fix myself *my way* over what God had planned for me. Spiritually, I had to admit that I couldn't do this on my own—and for me that meant total surrender of control for a complete makeover from the inside out. I love how Roy Lessin puts it:
"Hope encourages the heart to move forward through the trials of today, it shines a light of assurance into the darkest of places of uncertainty, and it places secure stepping stones upon every river that needs to be crossed."

This is a nice picture of hope, isn't it? As if we are hopping from one stone of grace to another, landing on the solid rock of truth. We then pause to focus on the next rock, catch our balance, and bravely step again. Hope encourages the heart forward, friend.

When you are in a pit, it's hard to reach out. It's hard to know how to change or to even wrap your mind around the fact that you need to change. Can I get a witness here? It's not easy to reach out for help. It's the most difficult to admit there's a need. Some changes seem tall like giants if made all at once. That's why we are taking this a step at a time. It took me years to write the letter to myself, but each time I read it (and I still do from time to time), I receive more and more healing.

Making It Real

Make a list of how you feel or think about yourself right now. Then research a few verses to see if your perspective lines up with how God sees you.

_____

_____

_____

_____

_____

_____

_____

_____

_____

Kickstart Action Step

I went first; now it's your turn. Write a letter to your younger self. It will kick start the hard part of your heart—to see yourself not only as others see you but as God sees you.

Prayer

Lord, I need You now. I am in desperate need. I'm in the middle of a mess and feel I'll never see the end of it. Honestly, I need to feel Your embrace on the inside of me. You know all that I need, but I feel so broken; I don't know what I need most. I want to see myself as YOU see me. I am blind to Your deep love for me, and I want to know YOU as you know me. Help me to want the best version of me. Heal me by Your grace and mercy. Show me what You love about me, and show me how to love myself. I need Your help to accomplish this. Help me in the way that only You can. I surrender my all to You. I need YOUR hope to get me through. I want to change my ways to love You most. In Jesus' name, Amen.

Notes

Chapter 7

The Self Hatred Hanging at the Back of Your Closet

Did you write your letter? If so, can you see how healing it is to tell yourself that you are going to be okay? Opening up with such authenticity is valuable beyond compare. When you set your heart wide open on God's altar, your "all-in" is on the line. To obey God, you have to surrender ALL areas of your life. Even the emotional memories of being 12.

But there's a hidden part of my closet I don't talk about much. It is hurtful to think about the regret of lost time and happiness when I remember how out of control life had become. Along with the emotional stress of carrying excess weight for years, there was also mental oppression. I was my own worst critic. I was so accustomed to carrying the weight of oppressive sin, that I didn't even notice it.

I'm not proud of who I was in those years. The mental game of perfection left a "cancerous worm" in my brain. Instead of letting myself be free of negative sentiments and receive compliments about my weight loss—or anything else—I let it feed my feelings of unworthiness. I felt I could never measure up to anyone…period. Especially God!

My negative self-talk went on and on for years. I made a "blame it all on me" list and checked in daily. Every day I spoke the same verbiage. Every night I went to bed with the same guilt. Something sick and twisted inside of me convinced me that I was unloved. Because of my past and excess weight, there was no possible way that God could love me. It was all black and white. If I caused trouble or ate something out of line, then I was "all bad." I had the "all or nothing" mentality in full swing. There was no way I would ever, ever measure up to my siblings or other skinny people. Openly, I would tell you that God loves *you* but *secretly* believed He could never love me. I felt I had messed my life up too royally to come under His free grace.

Thus, I entered adulthood, waffling in and out of insecurities, depending on my behavior in the moment. I was *pretending* to be the good Christian girl, with everything neatly put together. I believed that if you really knew me for who I was, you wouldn't like me. I chose to be a fake friend over being authentic with you. I avoided the camera, always loathed myself in private or even in front of close associates. My husband tried to build me up and encourage me, but he was married to me, therefore *he had to like me.*

The Blame Game

Chronic blaming is a form of emotional abuse. I blamed myself for not controlling my emotions, not measuring up to others, and subjected myself to verbal and emotional abuse and harmful habits over my worth. I somehow thought my words to myself didn't matter. I figured if I stuffed it down inside, then no one would know the difference.

My self-abuse left me with guilty feelings, inevitable poor self-esteem, and sabotaged relationships. But I took a first step towards change after a conversation I had with a fellow volunteer at a Christian concert. As we were talking, she shared how our words to ourselves matter, even if no one else hears them. **She went on to say that when you speak negatively to yourself, you disregard the love that God put inside of you and cast off that love. For you to think about yourself as unworthy or insignificant is defaming the love He said was good; it's the love He put in you at creation.** I looked at her at first and wondered how to stop the mental chatterbox from signaling fire alerts in my brain.

She admitted she also had a problem with self-degradation and wanted to change her behavior. So she made one small adjustment, which made a big difference. She changed her computer password.

What does this have to do with anything? Well, for a long time her password was "choppedliver." Then she realized how that phrase ricocheted negativity back to her every time she logged into her computer. She convinced herself she was actually chopped liver! Once she came to that realization, she changed her password in an effort to speak positive words to herself. Her story moved me to think differently about the way I spoke negative comments to myself.

I noted her idea on a piece of paper, stuck it in my Bible, and left it at that. I didn't take action on her suggestion. Her story moved me to want to change, however the only action I took was once again eating away my tears in a heaping bowl of my favorite ice cream.

At the time, I was your compassionate, funny, empathetic morning show radio co-host. I wanted to appear confident and on fire for God—the girl who had it all together. I rocked at leading mission teams and women's groups. Deep down in the dark shelf of my closet, I was faking it; I was an impersonator and a shallow person. *It was very hard to admit, that as I led others to see the love of Christ in themselves, I failed to see His love in me!*

One day it all came crashing down around me. I shared, via the open microphone, that I struggled with the negative voices in my head. There it was! I put my weakness out there for thousands to hear. My heart, wide-open, honest and vulnerable. After saying it, I felt so exposed and thought, "I've done it now. They will for sure hate me after this." I also confessed that it was something God was working on within me and trusted the Holy Spirit to heal me. But it didn't stop the enemy from pouncing on my vulnerability, like a ticking time bomb.

Well, that "bomb" exploded in the form of an email later that same day. A listener, who had heard my on-air confession, sent harsh, hurtful words, which flew off my monitor and straight into my aching heart. So much for being real.

The cursor spewed judgement and jumped on my last nerve. My mind went on the offense. I shudder to think how Satan had this perfectly timed. Remember, the enemy will stop at nothing to choke you out, especially when you are vulnerable. So subtly and deceptively, Satan twisted the knife a bit further. I absolutely crumbled at my desk. I had nothing left at this point and was hurt hard core. My mind and heart collapsed; my lungs had all the air sucked out of them.

Nevertheless, God, in His perfect timing, sent a rescuer of great grace. A long-time friend had visited my office that day and spoke life into me. It seemed it was a random visit, but God knew I needed help to pull out of the pit of despair. I was barely strong enough to lift my hand to Jesus. He said, "Janelle, you are not that person. You are who Christ says you are. You are His, and He is yours. Believe it over the lies of the enemy!"

I thought I was wearing God's armor that day. However, as I quickly found out, it can chink in one shot. My *real* friend did something I didn't have the strength to do. He clicked "delete" on that toxic email, then wrote out this verse with a black Sharpie: "Let no corrupt word proceed out of your mouth, but what is good for

necessary edification, that it may impart grace to the hearers."
Ephesians 4:29

In doing so, he spoke the love of Christ to me and removed the thorn from my aching side. "Do not let any unwholesome talk…. come out of *your* mouth, Janelle!"   God's voice boomed loud and clear, the words virtually jumped off the paper. I am a child of God! I should not tear *myself* down, up, or sideways! God WAS doing a grace work in me! Why would I put that under the enemy's feet and let him tromp on my self-esteem? I wouldn't!! I couldn't cower in fear anymore!

In that moment, God set me free from the hand of the enemy through His wonder-working power. I privately repented to God about how I had left my mind's door open to attack and had believed Satan's lies. I had denied God's truth about my worth and looked to man's opinion over God's. Ouch.

I still wince when I think of how I grieved God with those negative thoughts, but I'm so grateful that He loved me anyway and drew me into repentance. I wish I could say the words of the email disappeared from my brain immediately, but they didn't. I had to work each day to keep my thoughts captive and positive. When those old feelings creep back up, I repeat the words from Ephesians 4:29 that set me free that day. I kept the truth of God handy and ready to activate when needed.

You have the power of life and death inside of you. God can tame your tongue toward yourself and others, but you have to choose to let God show you His love for you first! You have to receive the gift of redemption and the huge value that God has placed on your life!

You might think you've asked God for help and deliverance, but the trashy self-talk has caused a barrier between you and Him. And nothing is more detrimental to a relationship than false accusation. We need to think carefully about whom we blame and the guilt we take on.

Who's Judging?

Matthew 7:1-5 says, "Judge not, that you be not judged. For with what judgment you judge, you will be judged; and with the measure you use, it will be measured back to you. And why do you look at the speck in your brother's eye, but do not consider the plank in your own eye? Or how can you say to your brother, 'Let me remove the speck from your eye; and look, a plank is in your own eye? Hypocrite! First remove the plank from your own eye, and then you will see clearly to remove the speck from your brother's eye."

Here, the word *judge* means "distinguishing between something positive or negative." It means to separate. It assumes an intelligent comparison. However, intelligent comparisons aren't what we do very often. There is a big difference between the judge in a courtroom and our own inner judge. The judge in a courtroom hears all sides, considers the evidence, and makes a fair judgment. Our inner judge quickly wants to settle the issues, often taking on blame that isn't ours to assume.

There is a big difference between the judge in a courtroom and our own inner judge.

If you are condemning yourself, you will naturally condemn others. If you are downplaying your gifts or abilities, then you are trying to gain significance in man's eyes. These are heart attitudes and is not godly behavior. I realized each negative that I spoke or thought about myself gave the devil a foothold to overpower my mind. My friend's negative keystroking reminded me I was locked out of my own courage; I had to make a hard change. Oh, what traps we get ourselves into, but what a Savior we have! He takes away all our negativity and replaces it with His amazing grace.

This Means War

Shame and guilt are ultimately the negative demons that have claimed your closet space. You can't see it, but you can feel it. The enemy has dressed up like a scale, a pretty size six dress that spews condemnation to you, or those jeans that once said "sexy" to you. Hanging at the back of your closet, these items whisper "you will never be… enough." You will never measure up. You are abused, you are used, and an outcast. You are the reason your spouse left you, you are the reason your children are rebelling, and you are the reason you haven't gotten into that dress, yet. You will never be acceptable in God's eyes.

Sorry for playing the devil's advocate here, but he comes only to steal, kill, AND destroy… **It's time to fight back!** The accuser says those things about you because he knows your identity is in Christ. But he also knows you've put your armor down—if only for a moment—trying to fight your battle on your own. He's after you because he is getting back at God and wants to keep you living in the pit of your past sins.

Living Free from the Negative

How *do* you live free from your past? You can't forget where your heart has been. What does freedom from an addiction really look like? How do you live in freedom from a life-long crutch? To start living free, you must take the first steps:

Establish safe and healthy boundaries. Eliminate those "triggers" that you run to. For instance, you have that "go to" snack that is either salty or sweet, specific examples are chips or ice cream. If you just had one bite, you convince yourself you can stop. Your mind thinks you are strong enough to resist, but your willpower chooses otherwise. Keep them out of your house! Taking precautions with those triggers lessens the chance of your temptation.

Guard your newly cleaned closet from any toxicity (new or old). Guard your heart. You overeat when under stress or pressure, upset or emotionally disturbed. When you feel the need to unload your feelings onto a food, there's a root issue. You will have to unlearn some bad habits and replace them with better choices. Run to God when tempted, no matter the situation; He will help you out.

Surround yourself with honest accountable people who will lovingly help you when facing trials or temptations. Communicate your health or fitness goals and be open with your struggles and insecurities. If you have someone to talk to about it, it brings you out of the emotional isolation that food traps tend to keep you locked in.

Remember you are going to be better when we get this little closet project finished. I promise you. You are going to be more whole and liberated like you never thought possible, super-charged to live free with joy as your crown.

Do what you can to prevent negative thoughts from re-entering your mind, soul, and most importantly your heart. Henry Cloud, a well-known Christian psychologist and author, explains something like this in his book *Boundaries for Leaders*. He calls it "learned helplessness," continuing on to say:

"It's shaped by the three p's of negative thinking patterns about ourselves by the opinion of others it becomes our own personal chatterbox. This negative self-deprecation brings self-hatred and replays ongoing failures that causes some intense software malfunctions in the brain to allow the negative labels to seep back into our minds and therefore never release negative expectations. A negative chemical spews into our lives, causing an attitude of failure everywhere we look." God's voice calls you out of hiding, and negative chatter keeps you a prisoner.

Perhaps you can identify with some of these negative thoughts:

❖ If I were skinnier, people would like me more.
❖ If I were thinner, I would be a better wife and mother.
❖ If I were lighter, I would feel better about myself. I would smile more.
❖ If I were a skinny girl, God would love me more.
❖ If I were smart like my sister, my dad would love me more.
❖ If I met my goal weight, I could boldly share my faith.
❖ If I were skinny, I would do more work for God.
❖ If I could just lose some weight, I would be able to do anything and everything.
❖ If I were thinner, all my problems would go away.
❖ If I were thinner, my pants wouldn't create my overwhelming muffin top roll.
❖ If I were skinny, I would have a closer walk with God.
❖ If I were a better Christian AND skinny, God would bless me more.

The struggle is real. How do you turn off the chatterbox in your mind? We all need balance in our life-plans, our life-hacks, and our life...all the way around. The point is: we each must deal with our own issues. My way of thinking won't necessarily fix yours, but it *is* best to consider how you see yourself versus how God sees you.

When you see His goodness in your life, you can freely approach your closet with gratitude. This outfit of surrender looks different for each of us. However, every problem needs a different perspective to battle it. If you are overweight—and no method or diet is working for you—then it is time to tweak your habits. Same goes with how you see yourself. When you let God deep clean the cluttered shelves of your mind, it will give you more encouragement than you could ever get from anyone else. No one knows your story like you and God, and He will honor your obedience and renew your hope.

Making It Real

As you come clean before God, His forgiveness will wash over you. When you give it all to Him, he will give you the desires of your heart. YES, He cares deeply about your health—including the emotional and mental aspects! God wants to dwell in a healthy temple while you're here on earth.

So be of good cheer my friend...you are going to be okay! You will be MORE than okay. You will be a new creation. You will survive! You will be better, not bitter, assured of your right relationship with God. That is hope at its ultimate level! There are ways to experience hope and freedom now! God hates suffering. You have a choice to ask God to help you out of your pit of despair or wallow in the sin you have allowed to infiltrate every part of you.

Think About It

Real life will present you with many opportunities to choose. Direction, meals, time, money, investments, and so on. God can quickly take the sidelines in the business of your busy-ness. Before you know it, He gets crowded out again. With no decision comes no action. With no action on truth, then no repentance. You end up right back into the negative tornado of your past pain. This is a bottomless pit of emotions and drama. The path through addiction is difficult and painful but can be overcome a step at a time, all the while holding the hand of Jesus.

It's not easy to do, and yet here you are doing it! As you continue this journey, the Lord will continue to give you peace, hope, and everything you need for every step you take. He is the one who knows you best! He created your heart, soul, and body, and He knows the kind of care you need. He has already promised to never leave you nor forsake you!

Life is too short to be stuck in the struggle for freedom. What are you longing for? What has been knocking on your heart's door to freedom? There's a desire that has captured your mind and heart. Don't be so scared that you don't even try. Don't give up! You are stronger than you know.

Why? Because Jesus is at the right hand of God praying for you. "Who is he who condemns? It is Christ who died, and furthermore is also risen, who is even at the right hand of God, who also makes intercession for us." (Romans 8:34 NKJV)
Remember, Jesus didn't give up when it was the hardest for him. So press into His endurance. Put your weaknesses on the cross and leave them there. Remember: **your future victory is greater than your present pain**. As the Apostle Paul wrote in Romans 8:18:
"For I consider that the sufferings of this present time are not worthy to be compared with the glory which shall be revealed in us." (NKJV)

Kickstart Action Steps

Journal all the good things God has revealed about you as you read this chapter. Be showered in the lavishness of His love!

1. Who do you need to forgive?

Prayer

God, show me where I have been bitter over better. You can't tolerate bitterness, so please show me how I can overcome this blame that eats away at me. You don't sing anger and condemnation over me, but love and faithfulness. So I choose to say that You love me, are healing me, and giving me a kind spirit towards myself. Strip me away from my shame, anger, resentment, and pride to birth a gentle spirit. Forgive me for letting this bitterness in my heart poison my relationship with You. I see now how I've turned away from You and towards this deadly sin. I now give You space to work again in my soul and mind. Remind me again how Jesus died for me to have perfect grace and mercy. Help me to be joyful in this time of healing instead of holding to regret and loss. As I cast off this burden upon You, please take care of my heart. Help me to do what I can't do, Lord, and perceive the new cleanliness inside of my chest. Heal me in the parts of my heart that seem so empty and hollow. I let go of all the ungodly words that are not of You. Bridge the gaps of intimacy and flow Your grace into my mind. Thank you for loving me as only You can. Amen.

Notes

Chapter 8
Living Forgiven

Before we go any further, I want to say I'm proud of you for

cleaning your closet. It's necessary to make room for the new thing that God is doing in you. And now it's time for the next step towards God's healing and your own personal breakthrough: Forgiveness. As you learn to forgive on all levels, there are a number of things you need to do each day.

Be Honest

Honesty helps more than you realize, even if it's only between yourself and Jesus. Honesty doesn't hurt you more, it heals you best. And if you were to be honest right now, you're likely thinking, "What will make this time different from the other 1,000 Monday morning attempts at the diet game?"

It sure feels the same in this wilderness, as you stand in the blowing sand and hot temperatures, with no oasis in sight. I know... I've stood in that same place. If you truly want a transformation, you have to change the way you do things.

When you become 100 percent honest with yourself, others, and God, you are going to be different. Your attitude will change, your heart will change, and hope will change you like it did me.

Get Rid of Past Guilt

Sweets, a.k.a. refined sugar, can take over a strong, sound mind and leave you in a pile of cookie crumbles. This notion runs rampant with those who struggle with food temptations. It's a powerless feeling that rises to the surface and quickly dominates your emotions.

What is your temptation? Is there something that continually gets in the way of your logic, dragging you back to that "one last bite?" When you succumb to food temptations, do you forgive yourself? Or do you allow guilt to overcome you, luring you back to that box of Twinkies?

It's easy to dance through the happy times, as we celebrate God's presence and give Him praise. When we go through tough times in our lives, Jesus is still with us. But what about those times when we know we have messed up and are afraid to go to God for fear of being condemned?

I found myself in that place as I cleaned out *my* closet. I would feel really guilty about something I ate, like the time I ate the whole "whatever" all by myself. Or it could have been when I thought, "Well, my kids are misbehaving right now, but this cookie will never talk back to me." And then I ate my hurting heart right to the bottom of the cookie jar. I was ashamed of my behavior.

It could have been any of those times, and it was tough to admit that to you. We can dwell on our past all day long, but that gets us nowhere and only memorializes our misery.

It's so important to knock that awful guilt right out of your life. Why? In a moment, you can go right back to that place. You don't even see it coming most of the time. That's why we need to have the armor of God on to protect our clean closets and let God wipe our old shelves clean. He wants to re-dress you and teach you what He thinks about you. He sings over you; you are an expression of His glory. And that includes what comes out of—or goes into—your mouth. This is a process, and it takes a wholly surrendered heart to come to a breakthrough.

So, friend, it's time to leave the guilt behind, cross over the river of grace, and take a nice long drink of Living Water.

Accept That Jesus Loves You

Jesus doesn't stand on the outside of our difficulties to cheer us on. Jesus is in the center of our lives, but we are the ones who step away from His grace and mercy by our choices. He is God who is our ever present help every minute of the day, in every need we encounter.

Think about this…you have a Father who loves you today. Not less when you powered down that package of Oreos or more because of those lettuce wraps you ate for an entire week. God loves you, and you can't change His love for you by what you choose to eat. God not only gives love, but He IS LOVE. And when you call on Him for help, He promises to help. But this is where you have to choose to get clean before Him. From there, He will clean you up and set you upright and steady, fresh to go the right direction. He is not keeping score of the number of failed weight loss attempts you stacked up in the corner of your heart. He doesn't care where you've been, but He does care enough to not leave you there.

Live on God's Terms

God will meet you on your turf, but He wants you to follow Him on His terms. When I read 2 Timothy 3:1-5, I was struck by the similarities between these verses that were written centuries ago with the world I was stuck in. It also made me stop and think about how this could be used as a call to action.

"But know this, that in the last days perilous times will come: For men will be lovers of themselves, lovers of money, boasters, proud, blasphemers, disobedient to parents, unthankful, unholy, unloving, unforgiving, slanderers, without self-control, brutal, despisers of good, traitors, headstrong, haughty, lovers of pleasure rather than lovers of God, having a form of godliness but denying its power. And from such people turn away!" (2 Timothy 3:1–5 NKJV)

I had to admit that I fit into the "dressing rooms" of unforgiveness, recklessness, and the love of pleasure…the whole list! And once I looked at myself in the mirror, I didn't like the spiritual reflection looking back at me. I knew that I had to hit the floor, cry out to God, and admit that I didn't know what I was doing with my health. It was time to come clean about how I abused my own body with excess weight. That was incredibly hard because no one likes admitting mistakes, especially when you know better. But my appetite for sweets continued to get the best of me.

Who are the people or what are the things you need to stay away from so you can move forward?

It was in the middle of my misery that God spoke through Paul's words in 2 Timothy: "And from such people turn away."

Read it again: ***"And from such people turn away!"***

Sound advice that I'm so glad I took to heart. Through the letter to Timothy, written to the church of his day, God kick started my steps toward freedom.

Take another look back to Paul's specific descriptions of the hard times that will be faced during the last days (verses 1-5). Who are the people or what are the things you need to stay away from so you can move forward?

Repent

Repentance means to change your way of thinking. It applies forgiveness to your life and respects the blood of Jesus as a life-changing substitute for your sins. It puts the sacrifice of Christ's blood in your place, reconciling your life back to God the Father. There's a supernatural exchange that happens when you ask for forgiveness and seek repentance. To break free and live free from bondage, you must think differently about forgiveness. Jesus died for all of your sins, including the sin of gluttony, lust, and fear.

I'm NOT going to list the mountain of sin in either of our lives. But what you need to realize is God cares about your physical, mental, emotional, and spiritual health. He cares for all your inside parts and outside parts. Living a life that is pleasing to Him means turning away from your sin and not going back to it. If you find yourself in habitual sin, thinking you can't do anything to change your behavior, you are wrong and are thinking wrongly about God. We were created to give Him glory and to walk in newness of life. We are called to take care of the bodies He so lovingly gave us. We are to take care of the garden of our hearts and to stay away from the things that cause damage and harm. We are to submit to His ways and share the gospel message of forgiveness. Our ultimate purpose is to wear His glory in our lives and have His glory shine through us. When we repent and ask God for forgiveness, He gives it immediately and restores us instantly.

It is our own guilt that keeps us from experiencing restoration, mostly because we are used to people not extending that sort of unconditional grace to us. And often we are the last ones to offer ourselves grace and forgiveness.

But when you fail to forgive yourself, you in turn reject God's forgiveness, and His light cannot shine its full brightness in you. Let God into your hurt. If you quickly sweep Him to the side again, you will continue to ignore His very present help in times of trouble. A truth I learned as I was losing weight was that I was ashamed to come before Him to confess. Deep down, I understood that He already knew my sins. But I didn't want to admit I was the problem. I was very deceived in what I believed about God. I believed He loved me less in those times when I was disobedient.

In the end, we can't be sane, functioning human beings unless we learn how to embrace forgiveness that Christ died for.

If you think about the renewal in your life when you first accepted Jesus, then you remember the good feeling you received when you cast off all your burdens. Forgiveness was set up for us to come clean for a reason. We, as humans, are inherently bent towards the desires of our flesh. There was a point in my life when I only thought that forgiveness related to "right versus wrong" conflicts in life but not to my physical appetite or internal strongholds. It was a life-changing day when I asked for God's power to invade *every* part of my life. Only God can impart His godly nature in us. Only His empowerment will draw us away from the deadly pursuit of our own pleasures and proud natures, away from the sin that can potentially keep us apart from God. This life of freedom can only be accomplished with the free gift of the Holy Spirit.

The power of the Holy Spirit is given to you when you personally invite Jesus Christ into your heart and life and repent of (turn away from) your sins. So submit yourself fully to allow the Holy Spirit to transform your heart and mind. He wants it all—from the inside out. Bottom line is, you simply cannot clean up good enough for

God on your own. You need a Savior. You need Jesus Christ to cleanse away your sins.

It's Time to Live Free and Forgiven

In the end, we can't be sane, functioning human beings unless we learn how to embrace forgiveness that Christ died for. Don't wait another day to put yourself on the clean-up list.

We all have "dark corners" in our closets. And those can be scary places to go. My past continually haunted me. I ate myself into a sugar coma over so many things. I slipped into an addictive lifestyle that kept me clanking in bondage and screaming for freedom, yet Jesus held the key to my chains.

We each need to go there to let Jesus in with His cleansing, illuminating truth and healing light. The lie that tells us we are unforgivable will plunge us into so much despair and fear that we will hide from God and fall to deception. If a sick person believes she is incurable, she won't let a doctor near her. Gradually her illness will consume her. It's leprosy of the soul and isolation from your very source of help.

Freedom in Christ is a great thing, but you have to let the holy transfer of God's grace change you to WANT to live free. Living free of what hinders you is the ultimate goal. But it's repentance that keeps you free. It starts with the everyday decision to accept God's forgiveness of your sins, to forgive those who've hurt you, and to forgive yourself.

Are you ready to be a freedom fighter?

Making It Real

Small changes get you closer to living free. Is there a piece of clothing (or more) in your closet that holds you back? Perhaps you bought a super-skinny dress as an incentive, but instead it looms as a constant reminder of your failures and is so unforgiving. Get rid of it! Instead, set up a reward for yourself when you break through with new healthy habits.

Think About It

You are an overcomer, so make a plan to help yourself succeed right where you are now. Take small actions to put your plan in motion. Practice every day! Think well; eat well; sleep well. Every stride you make towards your goal is a step away from where you were.

Take another look at how you see yourself. I know it's hard, but this chapter might have hit a new nerve. It's time to realize the beauty God sees in you. Keep in mind you have grace (remember chapter 5). YOUR SINS ARE FORGIVEN AND YOUR ETERNITY IS SECURE.

Kickstart Action Steps

1. Find a picture of the 12-year-old you, and put it with the letter. Thank God for who you were, zits and all.

2. Are certain negative thoughts on "repeat" in your mind? Use the verses you've journaled to continuously combat them.

3. When you think about yourself, you might have some regrets. What would those be? Choose to forgive yourself for each one on your list.

4. Read and write down Romans 8:1-2. It is packed with hope and truth about how to live in unity with the Holy Spirit in your current situation.

5. Journal these things if you want. Jot down the passage from Romans 8 on a sticky note to remind yourself of God's forgiveness every morning.

Prayer

Dear Father, I have sinned against You, and I need help, hope, and healing that only You can give. I recognize that Jesus' death on the cross is finished, and this forgiveness covers all my sins. I also believe You died for ALL of the shame, guilt, and sin that too easily entangled my heart. I confess I have been deceived. But I'm turning away from that old lifestyle and turning towards Your truth, Your ways, letting Your Holy Spirit have His way in my heart, mind, and soul. Lord, heal my inner temple where You live, and help me care for and to manage it properly. Remove my "stinking thinking" to make room for Your forgiveness and grace. I know You will help me get to where I need to be. Cleanse me from my secret sins. Show me where I don't live for You, and correct those ways within me. I don't want to miss out on what You have for me. I want to live free and in Your mercy. I love You, God. Amen.

Notes

Chapter 9

Purge Ill-Fitting Outfits of Shame, Blame, and Guilt

As a follower of Jesus, you must love Him more than anything or any one person. I did, or so I thought. But knowing Christ as my personal Savior and allowing Him to be Lord over my health was a different story. Further, I didn't let Him own my real identity until years later after reaching my goal. Still constrained with guilt and self-blame, a part of me still thought I had to earn my worth.

I assumed everyone was like me. The removal of shame, ill-feelings from rejection, and condemnation from perceived judgement of others can't be eradicated as long as we continually subject ourselves to the fear of man's opinion. I was locked tight in this private prison, and I was tight lipped by the shame of it all. But once I made the decision to grapple with my self-hatred, God gradually cut the chains of self-abuse.

I held the opinion of man in a higher regard over God's opinion. The yoke of people's opinion kept me crippled in fear! I was so blind to God's perspective of myself that I couldn't even consider receiving the grace for the shame, blame, and guilt that my reality had caused me spiritually. I said I was forgiven, but I didn't lay those weights down. In my head, it was my cross to bear because I had caused my obesity somehow. I internalized this negativity and kept my feelings in a locked box inside my heart.

Shame 101

So before we start to clean out this silent plague, let's define shame and why it's important to recognize it and cast it off. In her book, *I Thought It Was Just Me (But It Isn't)*, Brene Brown defines shame as "the intensely painful feeling or experience of believing we are flawed and therefore unworthy of acceptance and belonging."

How do you know if *you've* been victimized by shame?

- ❖ Shame feels like a black hole in your heart, or hurts like pain or an open festering wound that keeps spreading larger with each thought.
- ❖ Shame is the feeling of rejection.
- ❖ Shame is feeling excluded, not belonging or fitting in.
- ❖ Shame is feelings of self-hatred for yourself and believing that other people feel the same disgust about you.
- ❖ Shame promotes self-loathing and feels uncomfortable.
- ❖ Shame feels like solitary confinement, except you believe you deserve to be there.
- ❖ Shame is the feeling of embarrassment in exposing your flaws. The thought makes you want to crawl in a snake hole and die.

Sadly, I have felt almost all of these feelings on different occasions. A person walking under the spirit of shame carries the weight of the world on their weak and tired shoulders. These oppressive thought patterns are injured and twisted with lies. Every mistake is marked on your personal tally sheet of failures. You believe the sum of your past is *all your fault*. In fact, you may even be sorry you're breathing. You apologize for everything, even the weather.

I can recognize it easily now, but couldn't see past it then. It feels like a coat of iron worn constantly. You accustom yourself to the weight of it all. I mean, what's a few more pounds of shame? *Right?*

Naming Your Shame

When you name your shame, you identify painful belief (or beliefs) about yourself, without letting it define you. Approach each feeling as something Jesus has already given the death blow to. You don't have to suffer under the oppression of it anymore.

This self-evaluation is vital for the sole purpose that God wants to do a new thing in you. I must warn you, though, to get ready! It's about to get really rough all up in your closet...point blank with your shame, guilt, embarrassment, and the devastating effects it has on your life.

Let me give you a few examples of how I've named my past shame. (I mentioned a couple of these incidents in the letter to my younger self):

❖ In third grade, the school principal announced my track meet weight to the entire third to sixth grades. In a very loud voice, he boomed, "103 pounds!" I was in the third grade and, yes, still wearing plaid. And little ole me weighed in at that whopping weight—as much as the tallest, most athletic boy in the class. He was at least a foot taller than me; I was half his size and twice his width. At that moment, the humiliating number rang through the troops. Every fiber of my little girl feelings melted into a puddle inside of me.

❖ My high-school geography teacher called me the state capital of Maine: Augustus. My maiden name was Maine. Because I was so big, I was "appropriately" dubbed the capital city. My self-esteem, or what was left of it, was sacrificed for the sake of humor. Totally not cool to be the object of a teacher's put-downs and used as a geography lesson. I wanted to run far, far away.

❖ One summer, my dad tried to motivate me to lose weight, offering to pay me $1.00 for every pound that I could lose in high school. I believe his intentions were honest, and money makes a good motivator in some situations. But I didn't earn any money that summer. I learned the wrong lesson that summer: that love had to be bought. But the price was higher than I was willing to afford.

❖ There was an authority figure in my life who used to humiliate me in front of others. I did my job to the best of my ability; but when even one mistake was found, insults came hurling my way. That hurt more than you know.

Shame is important to discuss openly—to be brought into the light—because it eradicates confidence. I want you to know that touching this subject will get the enemy riled up. God wants us to live free of all chains and not be slaves to fear. Shameful memories might sting to recall, but it's worth pressing through to get God's full freedom. And think about how clean your closet will be when all your shame has been swept out!

Be very aware that the father of lies is subtle, crafty, and cunning. He wants to kill, steal, and destroy you and will stop at NOTHING to discourage this closet cleaning business. Satan wants you bound, hiding and cowering in fear and locked into your insecurities. He'll seduce you—lie by lie—laden with excuses until he takes you completely out. He is a manipulator and a master at what he does. Satan knows how to make himself look attractive, sweet, and smelling oh so delicious. I know. I've seen him at work in my own closet. So did Eve.

Let's go back to the Garden of Eden, shall we? To the day Eve was taken aback by the enemy. I hate that cunning snake. Eve was *deceived* by a half-truth about God. Then Adam *disobeyed* and followed Eve's choice. "Now the serpent was more cunning than any beast of the field which the Lord God had made. And he said to the woman, 'Has God indeed said, 'You shall not eat of every tree of the garden?' "And the woman said to the serpent, 'We may eat the fruit of the trees of the garden; but of the fruit of the tree which is in the midst of the garden, God has said, You shall not eat it, nor shall you touch it, lest you die.' "Then the serpent said to the woman, 'You will not surely die. For God knows that in the day you eat of it your eyes will be opened, and you will be like God, knowing good and evil.' "So when the woman saw that the tree was good for food, that it was pleasant to the eyes, and a tree desirable to make one wise, she took of its fruit and ate. She also gave to her husband with her, and he ate."
(Genesis 3:1-6 NKJV)

Eve didn't realize at the time that *she was already like God in every way*. It was her desire that led her into shame. Satan's evil strategy is simply to twist or distort the truth. When you accept his lies as truth, the toxicity of shame, blame, and guilt takes root.

In my closet, I used to have many stained outfits, tainted by embarrassing situations, humiliation, and shame caused by my own behavior and the actions of others. We have all messed up in one form or another. We all have piles of "dirty laundry," things we're ashamed of. We all have said things we regret. But as the Apostle Paul wrote in Romans 3:23, "All have sinned and fallen short of the glory of God."

We often assume that shame is reserved for people who have survived terrible traumas, abusive situations, and dramatic events; but this is not true. Shame hides in our darkest corners and actually tends to lurk in our familiar places including body image, identity, families, motherhood, parenting, finances, work life, medical conditions, addictions, age, religion, and the list goes on and on. You get the point. It powers up bad feelings and negativity. It infuses into our brains and sucks out the righteous life that God has planned for us. Everyone experiences shame because it's an absolutely universal emotion. However, the more you understand, the more you clearly see it coming—decked out in all its filthy, guilty garb.

There was a part of me that didn't claim my rights as a redeemed child because I couldn't get past the shame of my past. Therefore, I fell under the false assumption that I had to re-prove myself to God daily. Every day, I could never improve my thinking. Every day, I operated in defeat. That's not grace, that's a performance mentality that breeds more shame and guilt.

If you feel rejected, abandoned, abused, or victimized, there are some shame wounds lying dormant inside of you, silently debilitating your ego. Like a colony of termites hidden in the foundation of your spiritual house … in the dark part of your framework, they feast. Slowly munching away. The pests multiply and consume everything in their path. They exhibit group intelligence, reproduce, and grow to be a dominating force from within. They invade every square inch of mass available as their territory. They have scouts that strike out and seek places to build new nests. This is the worst kind of destructive, hidden enemy, leaving nothing but a skeleton behind a false facade.

I love how author Brene Brown explains it: "The subtleness of shame lies deep within you and can whisper false deception. Shame is all about fear so we must tackle the root issue of how your shame was born. Shame is about the fear of disconnection. When we experience shame, we are steeped in fear of being ridiculed, diminished or seen as flawed."

When shame shows, it exposes your disconnections with worth and acceptance. You become fearful in social situations and become ridiculously awkward emotionally. And though I came out of my growing-up years alive, I always felt like I would never fit in because of my weight. The shame I carried eradicated every shred of confidence I ever had, and there wasn't much to start with. Because I lost sight of my self-worth, I didn't believe my life had any value. At the time, I never knew or realized the deep love of my Heavenly Father.

Have You Fallen Prey to False Humility and Pride?

What is false humility, you ask? It is a self-defeating mindset and poor self-image or evaluating oneself too negatively. You may catch yourself saying things like: "I'm a failure," "I'm worthless," "I can't do anything right," or "No one likes me." It's the tendency to be self-despising or to belittle oneself, to be self-deprecating around others, excessively modest due to feeling inferior, useless, or unworthy. You may feel preoccupied with anxious concern for yourself and can't focus on others. False humility makes you a people pleaser, doing whatever others want, regardless of what's right.

Perhaps you are overly dependent on what others think, lacking prudence to think and judge rightly. It's feeling fearful of correction and feedback because of low self-worth or poor self-image. You may also lack self-assurance, initiative, and assertiveness.

Pride is defined as "thinking too highly of oneself, to have a puffed-up view or over-inflated opinion of oneself. It could include vanity and vain-glory—the excessive display and boasting in one's appearance, qualities, abilities, and achievements. Self-centered, self-seeking, and selfish, concerned chiefly or only with yourself and your advantage, to the exclusion of others. Selfish ambition and the drive to get ahead of others at their expense. Unteachable, refuses correction, resists feedback, treats others as inferiors or unworthy of care and concern. Domineering and overbearing, too demanding, too opinionated, too outspoken, too assertive."

I don't know what your demons are, but everyone has a few that need to be purged. I found myself dabbling in each of these prideful acts at one time or another and dealt with many people who wore them too openly. So which of the two ill-fitting categories do you fit into: *false humility or pride?*

Enough Is Enough

In the deception of your mind, your archrival, Satan, wages war against you to ensure you never claim your inheritance in Christ nor walk in His newness of life. You become spiritually paralyzed. Let's not forget that, as a person who knows Christ as your Savior, you are a blood-bought, redeemed child of the King. You MUST NOT forget the eternal connection of forgiveness and repentance from the hill of Calvary. Don't forget when Christ said "It is finished," that included shame, too! You CANNOT forget that you are worthy because Christ in you has made you worthy!

Jesus gave the shame of the world the FINAL DEATH BLOW! That's why Jesus took your place … to take the unworthiness, guilt, and shame to the grave. Jesus didn't die for nothing. He died for ALL of your sin, ALL of your deceptions, ALL of your guilt, ALL of your shame, ALL of your humiliations, ALL of your embarrassing situations, and ALL of your bad choices!

Set yourself free today. Get out ALL those filthy rags of unrighteousness and put those hot buttons to rest. Better yet, cast them out of your life for good. Douse the enemy with a big old tank of gasoline and set his den of lies ablaze.

Making It Real

I've been where you are right now. I've been the girl confused and shaking with fear. I was the one who wondered about true love and doubted God's love. I tried and tried to come clean on my own. I've fallen apart on the inside and questioned God about why He didn't rescue me when I couldn't rescue myself. I was the one who disrespected the good work that God tried to bring into my life. I've ignored the Holy Spirit and danced with the enemy oh too long.

Now it's your turn. Let yourself be washed again and again in the righteous blood of Jesus. He died for you to live free from the enemy's web of deception. Jesus died so that you could have a new life and have it abundantly! He died so that He could immerse your life with joy, peace, and happiness. He died for all the past shame that haunts you to this very day. Your shame and guilt are not bigger than Jesus. The grave where your shame and guilt have tried to bury you couldn't contain the power that rose above it all.

The weight of your shame was not heavier than the cross carried up to Calvary. The inner wounds of shame were punched by nine-inch nails. The love of Christ covers a multitude of sin!

Remember: You are worthy, you are forgiven, and you are redeemed—just the way you are right now. You are loved by the Creator of the Universe. You are not alone. He is for you! Proverbs 4:23 reminds us, "Above all else, guard your heart, for everything you do flows from it." (NKJV)

Quite a sobering thought, isn't it? ALL of your issues flow from your heart, so instead of blaming everyone else or your circumstances for your shame ... look within and examine your own heart. Do a self-evaluation and determine your shame triggers. A regular heart check-up is absolutely vital to your spiritual health.

Receive God's forgiveness. Jesus is your reconciliation. This act of forgiveness is not letting your offender off the hook. Forgiveness is simply the decision to not hold one's sins over his/her head, making that person pay for the hurt and pain he/she has caused you. It releases you to be free from the shame you have suffered. Let it all go.

Kickstart Action Steps

James 5:16 tells us to confess our sins to each other and pray for each other, so that we may be healed. The earnest prayer of a righteous person has great power and produces wonderful results.

1. Confess all the shame, offense, bitterness, lust, greed, envy, anger, and indifference. Who do you need to forgive and give grace to?

2. Confess all your wrong thinking about yourself. Nothing crowds the good things out of your closet like this kind of junk.

3. Forgive yourself every day. Scripture teaches us repeatedly to forgive others as we have been forgiven. Repetition teaches us to give grace—freely, lavishly, without strings attached. Forgive abuses and offenses of your past and those who have made you feel bad about yourself. Then forgive yourself for holding these chains of shame and guilt.

Prayer

God, we know that You are bigger than the monsters of shame and guilt in our closets. Right now, in the name of Jesus, we bind the enemy from entering into our thoughts, attitudes, personalities, decisions, souls, and minds. The enemy has no place where You already are. So we claim Your authority over our lives, and we claim the blood of Jesus over the areas where shame has taken root. We ask that you do a holy evacuation of the awful thoughts that scroll through our minds and cleanse us from this unrighteous behavior. Help us practice good thoughts every day, all day long. Your word says to take every thought captive. We claim victory over our shame through the blood-bought sacrifice on the cross. We are not who we once were because we have been changed by the power of the blood of Jesus. We praise You for the redemptive power of Jesus. Give us a forgetful attitude, and change the way we see ourselves as well as Your hand of healing in a more powerful way. We love You, God, and thank You for ridding us of the things we can't even bear to bring before You. Take sin, evil, and all addictions far away. Let us never return to the desire of it. Amen.

Notes

Chapter 10
Your New Identity Demands a New Dress

Have you ever shopped for a dress or outfit for a special occasion?

When you find what you are looking for, you know it. Your friend and shopping buddy (of course, we should always go shopping in pairs) says, "That dress…it's SO you!" It looks good on your unique body shape. It's complimentary to your shrinking figure, makes you look younger, smarter, or matches your skin tone. When this magical moment happens in the fitting room, you are victorious! And you purchase the dress, guarding it carefully all the way to the register so no one can snatch it from your grasp.

This fitting is to clothe the outside version of you, and I truly believe God delights in giving us those joyful moments. But, what about the inside? God desires you to be a woman of beauty, dignity, and strength from the inside out. Your true essence and "look" should come from the knowledge of who you are in Christ, not from a designer label—no matter how pretty it looks or the size on the tag. If you follow Christ with your whole heart, your reflection will be far more stunning than the finest couture dress on the Hollywood red carpet. His light and beauty will radiate far more brightly than the most brilliant jewels. While clothes are necessary, they don't make your inner image. That's God's business.

I Said Yes to the "Dress"

In 2013, my total weight loss was 132 pounds. It was the lightest I had ever weighed. You'd think it would have been a victorious day, but I couldn't give myself permission to celebrate. I had too much on my mind. With my husband's blessing, I quit my full-time job, giving up the financial security it brought to my family. Now God was about to rock my world with a completely new perspective. I chose to trust Him for His plan, with the vision to begin a mentoring ministry to help hurting and oppressed women overcome shame and weight issues. I didn't know all that God had planned; I only knew He had a plan.

My friends and colleagues offered many "atta-a-girl" pats for following God into His next step on my journey. I appeared confident in my decision and had some goals in mind when I resigned. My old job was like my favorite sweats—comfy and familiar. But changing into this beautiful new dress God had for me? It was exciting, but oh so daunting. Perhaps you can relate.

But something supernatural happens when you invite the Lord into your situation. You give God permission to enter where you dread to go. Believe me, I *could* still think of myself as overweight and hide in my baggy, oversized clothes. But I encourage you to embrace the beautiful, becoming new outfit of His grace. In order to do that, you need to release what holds you back. It'll take fights through fearful tears and a stubborn heart. But eventually something will shift inside, and you'll be better for what's ahead. Looking back on that year, I couldn't have anticipated all the Lord was going to do. And I pray the same for you, beautiful friend. You will have doubts as you enter a new season of self-discovery, but I encourage you to say yes to the new "dress" God has for you.

It's Your Turn to Twirl

God loves you, and everything He says and does is out of love for you. Scripture says we are made in His image. Have you ever thought about how you were created? God loves you so perfectly; you are fearfully and wonderfully made (Psalm 139:14)! Psalm 139:10 speaks of a holy God who wove you together by His hand of perfection for the purpose of reflecting His nature on earth.

The Christ connection is all the identity you need to have confidence, security, and full trust. The cross proves your worth. Jesus' blood is the best I.D. card you can receive. Jesus validates your purpose, which is to live in the redemption of the cross and do the anointed work of God. You are *His* before you are anything else.

Your identity MUST be founded in God alone. The world teaches worth measured by careers, dress size, square footage, or the numbers on the scale. You call it a mid-life crisis and buy a convertible and drive it from coast to coast to feel accomplished. Or perhaps you settle for a cheaper version, with a new haircut or highlights. You post it on Instagram and BAM! But then.... it's over, and you're over it. You coped, for that moment, anyway.

Dear friend, let me tell you that in my deepest cravings, nothing has *ever* compared to the satisfaction of walking in obedience and turning all my affections toward God. Even the unreachable "thing" I sought for significance was wholly met by touching the hem of His robe.

If your identity is wrapped up in anything other than Christ, you are giving too much control to it, and it will quickly dominate your life. That's not freedom. It's slavery, a mentality that will get you nowhere except the fast track back to your personal prison. It's a depleted mindset found in a pint of cookie dough ice cream.

Don't miss the beautiful vision God has for you. So go ahead…take a twirl and bask in the beautiful reflection of Him in you.

Beautiful in His Time

God's changes are a difficult process, I know. But please let me encourage you that it's worth it all. In the discovery of God's best, I am *still* learning who I am in Christ.

God looks at each of us with His beauty filter by His grace, mercy, and by His perfect Love. He sees us as a work of His own hands. We are His workmanship, His poetic statement, His craftsmanship, and His glory. We only need to measure our heart to God's heart. Man will always compare and point out failures and shortcomings. Humans put unrealistic expectations ahead of God's opinion. The lies and twisted truths of this world can only leave us with a mutilated self-esteem and leave our souls dead on the inside.

The world's picture of beauty leaves us feeling empty, worthless, with the feeling we have to compete to get God's attention. God will never compare His children. He has enough grace and love for all of us. You are a daughter of the King.

Your striking "dress" of God's grace is woven with His loving thoughts of you:

❖ I don't just tolerate you; I have adored you since I created you!
❖ I made you and know your name. I want you.
❖ Since the day I first thought of you, I have longed for you.

- ❖ I have been waiting for you to see your self-worth in Me alone.
- ❖ I kept knocking with love every time you came near with your tears.
- ❖ I never remembered the shame you hid in the dark corners of your closet.
- ❖ I've loved you with an everlasting love.
- ❖ My love for you has never changed.
- ❖ You are My daughter.

Ephesians 5:1 says, "Follow God's example, therefore, as dearly loved children…" You must remove the negative apparel you wear—the ways you failed or what you are or aren't. As I wear God's forgiveness and am robed in righteousness, I like to visualize my new Christ-centered attitude as a sparkling tiara upon my head. Isn't it becoming? Perhaps it seems silly, but it's how you are seen through the eyes of Jesus. We are created in beauty for His pleasure. It's your time to let God make you beautiful.

Making It Real

"Define yourself radically as one beloved by God. This is the true self. Every other identity is illusion." -Brennan Manning

A Holy God not only loves you, but wants you. You were made by God who knows your name and wants you and chooses you to be His radiant beauty. He wants to take your breath away. You know, there seems to be a fundamental need inside most people to be liked. Let me talk woman to woman here—I want you to know you are understood. God hears you and thinks you are pretty special!

1 Peter 2:9 says, "But you are a chosen generation, a royal priesthood, a holy nation, His own special people, that you may proclaim the praises of Him who called you out of darkness into His marvelous light…" Out of all the children in the world…God has "chosen you…

for Himself, a special treasure above all the peoples who are on the face of the earth" (Deuteronomy 14:2 NKJV).

Our heavenly Father's deep desire is to be close to you, to love you, to heal you, to draw you into Himself. But He will not force His way into your life. He will wait patiently, adoring you from afar. His love extends for your hand right now. His love for you is eternal and can never be taken away. If you are searching for His beauty in your life, know you are in the right place. His love is everlasting and effortless. Everything about you is God-breathed.

Many times, your reflection only glares back accusations. I get it. But when you see God's beauty in yourself, His brilliance and sheen will reflect in your heart's mirror. His beauty sets you apart from the world and makes you see yourself from His perspective.

You are not ordinary. Not who your parents said you were. Not who your employer or husband wishes you were. Not the plastic or edited versions we see on magazine covers. YOU are made perfect through the filter of Jesus and His work on the cross of forgiveness.

"I have loved you with an everlasting love; Therefore, with lovingkindness I have drawn you." (Jeremiah 31:3 NKJV)

God's beauty plan began in your heart before you were even born, and it is unfolding before your very eyes. God becomes enough when you want only His identity. With holy DNA in your life, you have all the love and approval you need.

Think About It

It's funny that we think we can push God to action. He's God, and He has His best "dress" in mind for you in His timing. His plans are established long ago, according to the gifts He designed within you in the first place. He even considers your potential, in light of all the insecurities that defeat you, cause you to stumble, and trip you up over and over. He's seen your entire journey—from where you have been to where you are going. He knows the purpose for which He created you.

Kickstart Action Steps

1. Study Romans 12:2
   "And do not be conformed to this world, but be transformed by the renewing of your mind, that you may prove what is the good and acceptable and perfect will of God." (NKJV)

2. Only God's grace can change the habitual and hurtful thought patterns and replace them with His grace and worth. Confess who you have believed or the thoughts you have held to. Does it line up with who God says you are? At His feet, we are gracefully transformed. Only Grace tells us the truth about who we are.

3. Journal what God tells you and how he shows His love towards you.

Prayer

Dear God, please touch my painful places to reveal Your beauty. Help me to understand Your grace-filled view of little me. There are a lot of raw places that still need to match with Your wholeness. Bring Your fullness to my hurts, and heal them with your Holiness. Lord, You are my Father. I am the clay, and You are the Potter. You give us opportunity to shine Your unique light and breathtaking views of love. Let my life represent You, my Craftsman Lord—my Maker and my Artist. May the works of my hands and heart be a reflection of the special gifts You have put inside me. May Your glorious design shine

Your glorious riches through my words, actions, and life. Let everyday be a celebration of Your amazing handiwork and every part of me reflect Your beauty to be Your holy, fearless, and wonderfully made design. Amen.

Notes

Chapter 11
Vulnerability: The "Perfect Fit"

"This, then, seems to be the work of the Spirit: to keep you vulnerable
to live and love itself and to resist all that destroys the Life Flow."
-*Divine Dance* by Fr. Richard Rohr and Mike Morrell

God's message of vulnerability was fitted for me as my pastor spoke
on brokenness one Sunday morning, illustrated through the miracle of
Jesus feeding the 5,000. Most of us are familiar with the young boy
sharing his small lunch with Jesus; the lunch was then used to feed the
masses. In Matthew 14, Jesus and his band of brothers performed one
of the most memorable miracles. It's easy to see how *impossible* the
situation seemed. The crowd was growing, and the disciples wanted to
turn them away. Jesus had a different idea and asked His followers to
feed them. They doubted. But, He blessed. And they witnessed that
little lunch grow, by their own hands, through the power of Jesus.
It was amazing, invigorating, and an "increased" faith moment.

Imagine, however, when the disciples gathered up all the
broken pieces from the leftover fishes and loaves. What a memory—a
total "WOW!" moment. Who wouldn't have been joyous at the wonder
of it all? But then I wondered if the men felt inadequate or insecure,
having held on to their fears instead of faith *in front* of the crowd (and
Jesus, for that matter). Was anyone embarrassed that Jesus asked them
to feed the crowd first, yet they didn't believe?

The Bible goes on to say that the disciples gathered the
fragments, but it doesn't say they ate the leftovers. They are human,
and after a long day of ministry, one could assume they were hungry.
Nothing builds your appetite like a good miracle! However, Jesus had a
purpose for the leftover scraps beyond a physical meal. He never
wasted an opportunity to teach His message of love and grace.

Honestly, I never thought too much about the broken pieces of
bread or the leftover scraps that the disciples gathered. What happened
to them? I believe that the gospel writer included that little detail for a
reason. And it was on this day the Lord taught me something new
about appetites.

Vulnerability Invites You to Be Brave

Let's pick up the rest of the story in Matthew 14:22-34. "Immediately Jesus made His disciples get into the boat and go before Him to the other side, while He sent the multitudes away. And when He had sent the multitudes away, He went up on the mountain by Himself to pray. Now when evening came, He was alone there. But the boat was now in the middle of the sea, tossed by the waves, for the wind was contrary. "Now in the fourth watch of the night Jesus went to them, walking on the sea. And when the disciples saw Him walking on the sea, they were troubled, saying, "It is a ghost!" And they cried out for fear. "But immediately Jesus spoke to them, saying, 'Be of good cheer! It is I; do not be afraid.' "And Peter answered Him and said, "Lord, if it is You, command me to come to You on the water." "So He said, 'Come.' And when Peter had come down out of the boat, he walked on the water to go to Jesus. But when he saw that the wind was boisterous, he was afraid; and beginning to sink he cried out, saying, 'Lord, save me!' "And immediately Jesus stretched out His hand and caught him, and said to him, 'O you of little faith, why did you doubt?' And when they got into the boat, the wind ceased. "Then those who were in the boat came and worshiped Him, saying, "Truly You are the Son of God." When they had crossed over, they came to the land of Gennesaret." (NKJV)

Peter was outspoken, a strong leader, and seemed confident. He was perceived as a man of integrity and purpose, and yet Peter was the only one who was willing to take a chance, to risk it all for the sake of looking foolish. Others in the boat thought Jesus was a ghost. There was no waiting line to step out of the boat. Peter stepped onto the water; the others watched.

How far did he have to go? How many steps? Had he eaten enough protein to endure this trek across the sea? Did he refer to the "disciples how-to" book before stepping out? Did he consider how foolish he would look to risk life and limb to satisfy the appetite to see for himself? We don't know these answers. What we *do know* is that Peter believed the voice of his Teacher, accepting His invitation to "Come." Peter was a simple man who was willing to risk it all to find out. This isn't for just those 11 people (brave or not) who watched. The invitation is open to anyone who reads this story.

Oh, how I hungered to walk on water, like Peter! But, sitting in the pew that Sunday, I felt more like those baskets of scraps piled in a dark corner of the boat: all used up, emotionally empty, and blind to what the Lord had next for me. With His help, I had done a huge thing, too. I was now at my lowest weight and was obedient to leave my job. But I was still desperate to hear from God about what to do and needed Him to renew my sense of purpose. I desired another confirmation, a divine green light that I, too, was walking towards Him and that He was still with me.

My only point of reference was my past. And as you have read, I attempted many times to fix myself…with plenty of failures, wounds, and scars to match. So it's interesting that at my lowest weight, I still needed a lesson in courage to receive all the Lord was leading me to do.

The day I heard this message, the Holy Spirit called out *my* insecurities. I realized that when it came to vulnerability, I was the weakest link in the chain. For years, I carried on strong like my extra weight didn't bother me. I tirelessly went through the motions but felt if I admitted my weaknesses and issues to others, I would sound like a complainer, a whiner, and very small-minded.

If you only knew how often I cried myself to sleep hoping that "tomorrow" was another day to try again, but yet failed over and over. In this message, I found hope to be used for God's ordained purpose. But first He had to rescue me from my feelings of loneliness and unworthiness. I gave myself permission to humble myself and be vulnerable.

That day I gained courage to invite myself into God's hope and let Him rescue me once again. I pictured myself as the 13th disciple; I stepped out of the boat beside Peter, walking into the light of God's giant love. That's how relatable our Savior is and how much He cares for you right now in your brokenness and fragmented past.

Jesus Is the Answer to Your Hunger for Purpose

God doesn't need your ability, He wants your availability. He has plans for your life in ways you can't see until you trust Him enough to step out in faith and find out. Yes, it might be risky and you might have fears of looking foolish in front of everyone, much like the disciples. But this could be the time when God is calling you to set sail for new territory.

God has big plans that include you but desires your *willingness* to be open and vulnerable. As you admit your vulnerability, you might feel as if you are weak-minded, insignificant, and cast aside. Rest reassured—from God's perspective, you are highly valued. God loves to reveal His nature through people, and He often uses His ordinary, broken followers to reveal His glory.

This is not easy. It's tough stuff and is layered in deep parts of your closet. Think of vulnerability as a connection point. When you lose your connection point with God, then you lose…period. Life's timelines are full of opportunities to achieve great accomplishments, both personally and professionally. There's nothing wrong with that. But if we aren't lining ourselves up with the purpose God intended, we will miss the miracles He wants to do *through* us.

Isn't it time for you to find out what God wants to do through you? As you hang on to your past, you cover up the very connections God can bravely use for another person's purpose. Through vulnerability, God can turn the scraps of your life into a meal for the next person who is struggling. That's not to say it will be comfortable or convenient.

It's easy to slip back into those insecure pockets of false security because of the fear of change or the hurts of our past. When making many changes however, God is growing you stronger in His nature!

God Knows Your Hunger to Be Changed from Scraps to Wholeness

Please allow me to be completely vulnerable with you right now. I had a lot of doubt as I grew into this new thing God was doing. Even though I knew God was leading me out of a full-time job, I had no inkling about what this decision would cost. There were many days I was insecure about this faith leap and thought I couldn't let anyone know how I felt. I was really good at hiding things because I viewed myself as useless, as if my purpose and identity was nothing but leftovers.

It's so easy to become hyper-focused on the little details of your misery, making it even easier to totally escape the bigger picture of God's divine plan. I was keenly aware of the memorial I had made of my past, yet couldn't see past my past. Perhaps you are like me and have already overcome so many changes, that you couldn't possibly handle one more. Maybe the load of food you have ingested or the consequences of sin is too heavy.

Vulnerability makes you brave enough to get out of your comfortable closet full of assumptions and perceptions and wear an outfit of FULL confidence and wholeness.

You are not too far out of God's reach or too much for His divine grace. You still have a purpose. And this makeover and closet purge can and will be used by God for His glory.

The fact remains that I could have given you a bullet point list of "how-to's" and rules, actions, and steps to lose weight. But I knew that this book wasn't purposed for that. There's already a wide buffet of options when it comes to plans, diets, and programs—just as there are Plenty of lies you've believed—hook, line, and sinker. Take Peter's example. He called out and said, "Lord, save me!" And immediately Jesus stretched out His hand and caught him.

Where was Jesus? Was he far? Did He call a rescue team? Did He call committees to help because Peter was too far out of reach? No, Jesus *immediately* stretched out His hand and caught him. But if Jesus was right there and saw Peter sinking, why didn't He intervene? He already knew how this whole scenario was going to play out. Come on, He's Jesus and knew it all! He sees into people with His divine eyes. He *wanted* Peter to be vulnerable to teach him confidence. Accepting help is one thing, but receiving grace is another.

Vulnerability makes you brave enough to get out of your comfortable closet full of assumptions and perceptions...

121

It Was Through Peter's Walk of Vulnerability that We See the Only Fix for Our Brokenness: Jesus.

He alone is the right LIFE-source. There's nothing more costly than becoming vulnerable in the Lord's presence. Once you meet Jesus face to face, it changes you.

This is the way God planned for faith to work. God wants us to trust Him for every answer in every need. Yes, He gives us plenty of systems and tools to help us in life, but He wants to be our only SOURCE of life. He is our ever-present help! I can't emphasize this enough! What faith offers is hope.

Hope is anchored in faith—and what faith we read about in Hebrews 11:1… "Now faith is confidence in what we hope for and assurance about what we do not see." (NKJV)

Cling tight to hope like an anchor, and God's Spirit will keep you afloat. But first you have to get out of the boat. Is this the day the Lord is asking you to come in closer and go deeper with Him?

Could this be the true miracle you have been looking for? Are you hungry to know Him in this way? Are you looking to be skinny and slim or healthy and whole?

When you are vulnerable with God, you will understand how He feels about you and where you have been. Believe me, He will connect with you if you have the desire to connect with Him.

When the Lord asks you to "Come," let Him have His way. Like a rushing wind, you can choose to go your own way or to stay the course of hope, with the true identity He has placed in you. I do understand this is very difficult, but you aren't in this alone. You can pretend and play dress up all you like. But when you realize God's purpose for your life, you are more willing to cooperate and live in harmony with Him. The results are life-changing and liberating.

You Need to Be Vulnerable with God About Your Doubt

Interestingly, as we look back at Peter's walk on the water, it's true he risked it all to get near to Jesus. Daring to step into your destiny looks bright and promising, doesn't it? But it's an individual journey, and you must CHOOSE to be honest with God in your struggles.

Like me, perhaps you have spent too much time in your "boat" of overwrought emotions. Friend, it's time to cast your "perfection disguise" overboard into the deep sea and be vulnerable before the Lord. Take it from me. I wasted too much precious time acting like I was OK and could handle things on my own.

From this story, we can also glean some insights into how doubt infiltrates the deep recesses of our closets. Our past wounds hold us back as a way of coping with imperfections and assumed weaknesses. Vulnerability can be personally powerful. You must get to the core of your authenticity to discover your real identity.

It took great courage to tell you that I lacked faith. After many years of looking to the scale, I lived only scraps of life due to an unhealthy view of myself. I was ashamed of my hypocrisy in saying that I relied on God but looked to any measure except grace to gain a new perspective for a healthy lifestyle. I also needed some insane courage to write my story and discover the vulnerable voice from within.

It's in your vulnerability that you can accept the whole grace that your Lord and Savior Jesus gives. In His tsunami of love, Jesus sweeps away negativity and the idol of false humility. After you understand the deep love of the Father, you can't help but give Him all your love back. The only way you can walk weightlessly on the water is when you allow all your sin nature and doubt sink to the bottom of the sea.

When I got vulnerable with God, I discovered that I am NOT the sum total of my mistakes, failures, attempts at losing weight, or the negative words I used to tell myself. I'm not just a better version of the "fat" person I used to be. I was worthy because of what Jesus had already done!

Vulnerability brings a newness by His grace. His GRACE mends the heart's broken pieces and makes you whole. Your destiny is defined by who you are in Christ...not because of what you did or didn't do. When God's love sinks deep in your inmost parts, you are able to feel His deep love. God's feelings about YOU will never change! God is at the end of every step you need to take.

Personal honesty and the acknowledgment of your doubt lay a clear foundation for God to work. If you want to get to the place of vulnerability, you must first be willing to name your imperfections, accept what you cannot change, and boldly face what you can.

The steps into your destiny are for the taking and are foundational in declaring yourself qualified. If you are like me, you might have thought there was no way God could use your broken life for good. You render yourself useless and without purpose, without even consulting God who made humans and restores perfectly. In this frame of mind, it's natural to fall to a victim mentality, feeling powerless to overcome your inadequacies, imperfections, and failings alone.

To set yourself free and live a life of purpose towards your destiny, you must learn to embrace your imperfections. This is the pathway to truly love yourself with all your quirks, dimples, wrinkles, sags, and baggage. In loving who God made you to be and walking in true humility and simplicity, you are walking with purpose.

The Miracle of the Cross Is the Beautiful Gift Behind the Scars of Jesus.

Your message emerges out of your weakness, brokenness, and emotional fragility. In accepting God's grace, you can embrace your imperfections. Faith begs us to be open and connect with others.

According to social media, it's the world's appeal to project a flawless and glorious life. However, in the wisdom of vulnerability, you can demonstrate to others that brotherly love draws an honest community of mutual struggles. There's restoration and reconciliation within hope-filled empathy with people. In other words, there is more hope in honest brokenness than in the pretense of false wholeness.

This is why I chose Peter as the center of this chapter. I dared to become vulnerable the day I created space in my heart's closet for the purpose of my destiny. I knew for months God was asking me to write this book, but I didn't want to open my flaws to you because of shame and my sin-scarred past.

Yet, it was in my heart-broken vulnerability with God that I understood this was my commonality in community. There were many imperfections, and God dared me to tell them. I'm not perfect in this. But this has been cathartic at best, and my life has changed dramatically. Not only has it brought wholeness into my life, it sustained my personal joy in writing. Learning from your mistakes prevents you from looking to your past.

Now, it's your turn to get vulnerable. I don't know where you are or what boat you have been stuck in. I don't know what empty baskets or pieces you have laid scattered in your spiritual closet. But I do know that God is here to help you. There's no weakness or insecurity too great that His greater grace won't cover.

God will keep you afloat and give you all the hope you need to live a victorious life. You will never measure up to God's standards; that's why you need Jesus. And now that you know that, you must tell yourself that you are just fooling yourself when you look to anything else but God for your standards in living a free life.

It's time to step out and live a life for the One who has set us apart. Step out to walk in the newness of Christ. Because we are living from the approval of Jesus, who gave us all the approval we need on the hill of Calvary, we can walk in the authority of knowing whose we are. We can live in the freedom of knowing the truth as God's dearly loved disciples and know what freedom looks like. John 8:31-32 says "Then Jesus said to those Jews who believed Him, 'If you abide in My word, you are My disciples indeed.' And you shall know the truth, and the truth shall make you free."

Making It Real

This weight journey, matched with your age and existing health issues, takes accepting what you can and can't control. Asking for help and allowing God to help you is vital to your success. He will give you the tenacity to endure, the strength to persevere, and the willingness to adjust as you go. In my experience, I have found He is patient and long suffering with each change and delights in teaching us how to live our best life.

Good health and honest living needs to be a continuous process, consistently cutting out distractions that detract you from living in total freedom. It's not "one-and-done." Through the willingness to be vulnerable, you will gain knowledge to make changes when needed. Every step requires more and more practice with focus and determination.

There's a new voice calling you. One that requires you to be strong, brave, and vulnerable. If it looks impossible right now, you are in the right place. That's where God likes to work a miracle. Ask Him to fill your empty places, your broken spaces, and the answers to your brokenness.

Remember there's no blueprint for your healing except you must believe that healing is found only in Jesus, not food! There's a brilliant light that appears in the distance that is whispering your name, "Come!" Join me as the "the 14th disciple" and discover what God can do with the hidden, broken pieces of your heart and soul.

Imagine Jesus is right next to you asking, "What can I do to help you today?" Then tell Him about any needs you have. He alone can lift your perspective to see the brilliant love that doesn't condemn but has died to set you free. He died so that you might live.

Let Him set you free by His grace that is sufficient for every last need! Remember, just as He was ***right there to help Peter*** when doubt came blowing in, He will be there for you.

Kickstart Action Steps

Read through Isaiah 43:1-8. Then journal the ways you sense the Lord is asking you to be more vulnerable. Let God's invitation to be vulnerable in His presence break through to your heart.
Here's what He is saying:

You don't have to be perfect. Come to Me empty and broken.

- ❖ I will turn your ashes into beauty.
- ❖ Only I can turn your sorrow into joy.
- ❖ The altar is wide open to see My grace.
- ❖ Anchor your hope to My mercy and grace.

Prayer

God, You have rewritten my life's song, telling me I am Yours and You are mine. Reassure me in this new beginning, and help me to see the light of Your love. You call me out on the waters to dare greatly into my purpose. I want to get up close and personal with You. I believe Your Word and how You see me over and above the doubts that come against me. There's no weapon that can be forged against this kind of faith. And Lord, keep my eyes on You. Call me out of this sea of insecurity and doubt, and bridge the gap between fears to faith. The cross proved Your worth for me. The power of the cross is alive in me. I won't be overcome by shame and guilt any longer. I will rise anew and with purpose to walk in humility and love. I thank You for Your mercy and grace. Thank You for Your presence. Thank You for the comfort and strength You give when I come to You. Help me overcome, Jesus. Amen.

Notes

Chapter 12
Put on God's Power Suit of Worth

You know that feeling of wearing a new outfit? You are happy,

feeling good about how you look, and see how your good health choices "earned" your way into this dress. Your smile says it all; life is good today, and you have nothing to hide. What wonderful freedom it is to "wear" your hard work!

But reflect upon where you once were (inside your emotional closet) to where you are at this moment. There could be some scraps of soured or tainted emotions which rise to the top of your heart right about now.

Emotions can either deter your life or determine your course. As a woman, you have a heightened awareness of emotions, and there are days when that section of your inner sanctum is messy and cluttered. Let's face it, women's brains are like noodles—where each wet, stringy piece is connected to a specific emotion, story, and feeling. You secretly carry your wounds and those of others.

And if you're like me, you wear those "emotional noodles" on your sleeve! Feelings will fool you; emotions become instant commanders. I hope and pray this very personal look inside your closet gets you in tune with your right and wrong feelings or reactions.

Mismanaged Emotions, Mismanaged Life

You're a sensitive person…I get it. You carry the world on your shoulders. When you finally get to church on Sunday, you pump your fists in victory shouts, only to be overwhelmed by the wave of Monday's problems. Again.

The fact remains, whether you feel good or not on any given day, your feelings stem from your own set of emotions and lack of self-worth. The choice is yours to "wear." You can let yourself be beaten down or decide to put on God's version of you. And relish how He uniquely designed you, from your brain down to those pretty little painted toes.

I've taken countless personality tests, and each has told me I'm "sensitive" and a "feeler." I used to be ashamed of that, but I've grown to be grateful for this gift. I'm always confused when I see both men and women who are out of touch with their feelings. It's as if their hearts and minds are like machines, robotic in nature, using logic to express their so-called feelings. I once worked with a guy who let everything roll right off his proverbial back. What? How!? Could a person feel that insufficiently!? But it was his way of dealing with life. And yet, I do have to acknowledge in my heart of hearts that I also take life in differently. This awareness helped me to accept myself. I've become keenly aware of the lack of self-worth born out of my mismanaged emotions.

Vacillating from a comfort eater to one who is now self-controlled, I had to walk this journey first-hand to gain a better perspective of my emotions and gain control of my response to food. Once I realized food had become such an overwhelming idol in my life, it changed my perspective. I addressed my response to food and took ownership of my emotions regarding it. In the management of my food behaviors, I learned I had the power of choice. As I overcame my will with good healthy choices, I subdued my desire to be comforted. Is it time for you to confess that you've thought wrongly about your relationship with God, especially in relation to food behaviors?

Untangle, Re-Sort, and Re-Organize Your Feelings

The truth is we all have self-esteem and worth issues in our lives. We were born with it. It's called original sin (in the spiritual sense). After all, life for Adam and Eve didn't come with a *Dummies Guide to the Garden of Eden*. The first outfit they put on after the fall initiated a chain reaction since day one!
Out of their shame came unworthiness.
"And they heard the sound of the LORD God walking in the garden in the cool of the day, and Adam and his wife hid themselves from the presence of the LORD God among the trees of the garden." Genesis 3:8 (NKJV)

When they realized their own shame, they tried to cover up! Oh they immediately knew wisdom alright. Their sin was apparent now, and they did what they could to cover their own skin. What happens next is indicative of their response.

They tried to blame and ignore … like nothing had happened. Seriously! How many of us have done the same thing? I've mentioned this before: the worst kind of food sin is the one done in secret. If hidden, it never seems real. And we blame everything and everyone. Except ourselves. Shame is easily hidden; blame is too easily cast aside and ignored. Over time, all this negativity has disastrous results on our worth and self-esteem.

As I took a long look at my own shame, it gave me great empathy. Shame is a gigantic animal to tame, however it remains hidden until it's brought to light and uncovered. Shame has to hide somewhere. That's the way it works! When we rise to the standard of God's worth, we can only compare our dysfunctions to the truth of His grace. I understand this might be a new perspective for you, so please hear me out. Adam and Eve knew the truth about which tree to eat from and not. *They knew.* Eve even repeated the truth to the serpent right before she took that infamous first bite. But it wasn't Eve's lack of self-control that Satan was after. It was her sense of worth; he simply twisted her desire to want what wasn't hers.

Adam and Eve were the most like God before sin entered their world. They had full knowledge of God in their perfect state. Then here comes the voice of discontent that slithered its way before the weaker emotional being—that carried the heart of God! Oh our wayward hearts!

Eve, you and I have been so easily swayed by deception. Adam knew it was wrong too, but didn't stop her! Regardless, the grace that entered into the Garden of Eden is the same grace that can enter your closet of misappropriated feelings and desires. Grace heals the pain that shame left in the soul. This healing makes you clean and whole again. You must discipline yourself to behave around deception and gain godly self-control.

Remember, Your Worth and Self-Esteem Are at Stake

I pray on this day your outfit changes to one of self-worth and confidence. What feels impassable right now will change if you let God's grace take over your wardrobe. I, too, missed the value

God had placed on my life. The many hurts over time damaged my relationship with Him. There was a heart blockage I couldn't get past. It wasn't until the Holy Spirit called me out of my closet of misplaced emotions, that I realized there were deeper root issues with my self-worth and wrong ideas about God. I'm not proud of those days and the way I acted, empty of confidence as a child of God.

However, as I received His full measure of grace, my issues resolved themselves. Jesus is once again center of my heart's throne. I submitted my life to simple devotion by living changed by His grace and as His much-loved child.

I am now walking outwardly in God's grace. Hiding out didn't work for Adam and Eve (or me), and it won't work for you, either. Drop your addictions that only feed your fears, and exercise your faith instead. God's love is beyond compare and lasts eternally—much longer than some sugar high. Setting right boundaries and healthy disciplines bring a bright light into your soul and a deeper understanding of who God is. The most important confidence you need is to live redeemed and to continually acknowledge God in all things. When you realize how big His grace is, you know GRACE is enough to cover all your complexities and insecurities.

Lay down those Snickers bars and exchange them for true worth.

There's no fear in moving on with your life once you secure your love back into Him. All it takes is to accept this gift and receive it in your heart. God loves you as you are right now and knows the future for you, too. In fact, He can't love you any less because He is the epitome, the originator, and the CREATOR of Love itself. He's not angry with you, nor is He setting any traps to tempt you. He yearns for you to ask Him for everything you don't have. Jesus said it right the first time! "I AM the Way, the Truth, and the Life." John 14:6.

God's grace earned for us on the cross what we could never do for ourselves. Daily we must rise above our sin issues or we will bend towards evil desires. But in distancing yourself from your sin nature, something wonderful happens. You start to care less about appeasing your own nature, and the desire to worship God becomes your focus. And then you gain strength to rise above the feelings that drag you down.

Where Comparison Begins, Contentment Ends

Measuring ourselves against each other brings either superior or inferior feelings—neither honors God. But as women, we tend to gain our self-worth by how we look—our shape, age, hair color, wrinkles, fitness level, etc. Nothing could falsely represent the radiance of Christ! Believers are spirit beings in human flesh!

This is your day to put on your outfit of obedience and live free of people's opinions. Lay down those Snickers bars and exchange them for true worth that has an intrinsic life-long value placed by God! It's time to put on your power suit!

Making It Real

Ask God what's in the way of your personal relationship with Him. Let God do a new thing in your heart. Let Him into your soul's closet and dress you in a new image. Watch as His renewed grace gives you a new confidence! Nothing is too hard for Him, and you'll never slip too far out of His reach. He can rummage through that pile of worn-out denim dreams. Don't weigh yourself down with discontent. Embrace your imperfections, flaws, and hang ups; allow Jesus to help you change! This is your new beginning. Now your charge is to live changed and love yourself like He does. I promise that once you get the bird's eye view of you, you'll never go back to the way you were! Freedom fits all too perfectly, friend. Talk about a new comfortable! It's all warm and fuzzy in our hearts right now! There's no room for judging either! Remember His GRACE:

God's
Radiance
Always
Covers
Everything

My journey is not your journey, but I uncovered my worst to help you achieve your best, with God's help. And I pray you will make room for God to speak to your heart and bring His peace to your soul.

I hope you've enjoyed reading this and will be inspired to live open to all God has in store for you. May you be blessed as the Spirit moves in you. Strive to see God in a fresh way with your new outfit of GRACE and the truest form of WORTH!

Kickstart Action Steps

1. Intentionally put on God's power suit each day. (Check out His armor in Ephesians 6:11-18). In order to do this, set aside your thoughts of unworthiness. Each day, take steps to re-train your brain to disrupt negative thought processes. Revel in the fact God loves you just as you are.

2. The battle for your worth has been won! Believe that His beauty plan begins in your heart today!

3. Consider the place these verses have in your spiritual closet.

   "But we all, with unveiled face, beholding as in a mirror the glory of the Lord, are being transformed into the same image from glory to glory, just as by the Spirit of the Lord."
   2 Corinthians 3:18

   "But seek first the kingdom of God and His righteousness, and all these things shall be added to you." Matthew 6: 33

"Finally, brethren, whatever things are true, whatever
things are noble, whatever things are just, whatever
things are pure, whatever things are lovely, whatever
things are of good report, if there is any virtue and if there
is anything praiseworthy—meditate on these things. The things
which you learned and received and heard and saw in me, these
do, and the God of peace will be with you." Philippians 4:8-9

How do these words make you feel? Write your initial thoughts
in your journal. In what ways can you clear out room in your
closet to let the glory of the Lord shine brighter? *What will it
take for you to put on your power suit every day?*

Lord, You are my Father. Let my heart respond to GRACE by my love!
I am the clay and You are the Potter. Help me make the most of every
opportunity to shine Your unique light and breathtaking views of love.
Let my life represent Your Craftsmanship. May the works of my hands
and heart be a reflection of the worth You have put inside me.

May Your glorious design shine through my words, actions, choices,
and my life. Take my life and let it be Yours! Let everyday be a
celebration of Your amazing handiwork, each part to reflect Your
beauty, every square inch and fiber of our being as an instrument of
praise for the marvelous redemptive work of Jesus. I am blameless,
shameless, and confident by the truth of Your Word. Empower me to
live free, a life of worth that is only found in You, Lord. I thank You
for this gift of life You have given to me. Amen.

Notes

Closing Thoughts

Sharing God's glory story with you has been a privilege I don't take lightly. I am alive today because of His wonderful miracle of hope. I pray this book inspires you to seek His purity in your life. Let's face it, you picked this book up because you needed an answer. I also pray God's grace solution works for you.

Perhaps you have put God back in place time after time, only to continue to fall from grace over and over. That's okay! He is still with you! Searching for answers is a journey and a long process. Over time, changes do happen. Believe today you have a choice.

This journey is one full of many victories, failures, fears, and tears. It's a hard-fought battle. So as I close, here are some thoughts to take with you:

- ❖ Your worth is not a number; it's measureless in the sight of God.
- ❖ With the Spirit at work, you have the power to choose righteousness.
- ❖ Use Christ-esteem, not poor self-esteem.
- ❖ Know Christ awareness, not self-awareness.
- ❖ Carry His easy yoke, not restrictive rules.
- ❖ Take second (and more) helpings of Grace, not a continual buffet of self-condemnation.
- ❖ Sing a constant chorus of God's praise each day, not continual cries of despair.
- ❖ Speak for God's glory for HIS RENOWN, NOT YOUR OWN!
- ❖ Live vulnerably; pride and perfection block grace.
- ❖ Embrace your imperfections and wear healing in a righteous way.
- ❖ Allow God's love to shine to others.
- ❖ Stop shaming and blaming! From this day forward, you cast off all idols of unworthiness.
- ❖ Stop the comparing! We will never be good enough to measure up, but because of Jesus we don't have to!
- ❖ Accept grace ... it is enough to cover your most heinous binge!

   Release your inner hurts and pain, and rest in His love!
It's YOUR time to let God make all things beautiful and bright! Let the healing begin! YOU are His treasure … and how He feels about you is not changed by how you feel about yourself. Your identity was worth dying for.

You were chosen to be His!

Welcome to your transformation!

About the Author

Janelle Keith is an authentic, tender, and compassionate voice devoted to God. She knows firsthand the struggle of making food behave over trendy food modification behaviors. Through her personal journey toward better health and struggle to find significance, God unshackled her life from the bondage of overeating. Through her experience, Janelle not only lost 132 pounds and downsized from a dress size 24 to 4, she also gained significant freedom from food and the need for approval.

Janelle has maintained half of her original body weight and is enjoying a healthy lifestyle of balance fueled by the grace and hope of God. She lives outside of Stillwater, OK with her husband Terry. They have two grown children and three grandchildren.

Keep up with Janelle at www.thejanellekeith.com.

I would like to thank my Street Team:

Patty Gilliland

Pam Worcester

Nancy Simon

Laura Whitfield

Jenny Wood

Stacey Husted

Sandra Chesterman

Tammy-Dawn Gibson

Tina Ahern

Julie Broussard

With special thanks to:

Amy Kirk, cover design

Dawn A. Estela, layout and design

Lori Twichell, publicity consulting

Brenda Belovarac, proofreading

Attributions

Chapter 1: "No approval can match what our Creator has to offer. God can't bless who you pretend to be!"
Attribution: Steven Furtick, Lead Pastor at Elevation Church, from the sermon series *Death to Selfie: Just Call Me Jacob*, August 2014.

Chapter 1: "Don't let your happiness depend on something you may lose . . . only (upon) the Beloved who will never pass away."
Attribution: C.S. Lewis
https://www.goodreads.com/quotes.

Chapter 3: "Rejection (or dysfunction) knows no bounds, invading social, romantic and job situations alike. And it feels terrible because it communicates subliminal messages of unloved or unwanted, or not in some way valued."
Attribution: Gerald Downy
https://psychology.columbia.edu/publications#/search/dysfunctions%20

Chapter 3: "We think sometimes that poverty is only being hungry, naked, and homeless. The poverty of being unwanted, unloved and uncared for is the greatest poverty. We must start in our own homes to remedy this kind of poverty."
Attribution: Mother Teresa:
https://www.brainyquote.com/quotes/mother_teresa_130839

Chapter 4: "Grace is the active expression of his love."
Attribution: Brennan Manning. *The Ragamuffin Gospel: Good News for the Bedraggled, Beat-Up, and Burnt Out.* Publisher: Multnomah, 2005.

Chapter 6: "Hope encourages the heart to move forward through the trials of today, it shines a light of assurance into the darkest of places of uncertainty, and it places secure stepping stones upon every river that needs to be crossed."
Attribution: Roy Lessin. Lessin photograph: Website for Roy Lessin @ Google Images.

Chapter 9: "defined shame as the intensely painful feeling or experience of believing we are flawed and therefor unworthy to acceptance and belonging."

Attribution: Brené Brown. *I Thought It Was Just Me (but it isn't): Making the Journey from I "What Will People Think?" To "I Am Enough."* Imprint Penguin Random House, 2007.

Chapter 9: "The subtleness of shame lies deep within you and can whisper false deception. Shame is all about fear so we must tackle the root issue of how your shame was born. Shame is about the fear of disconnection. When we experience shame, we are steeped in fear of being ridiculed, diminished or seen as flawed."
Attribution: Brene Brown. *The Gifts of Imperfection: Let Go of Who You Think You're Supposed to Be and Embrace Who You Are.* Hazelden, Center City, Minnesota, hazelden.org, 2010.

Chapter 10: "Define yourself radically as one beloved by God. This is the true self. Every other identity is an illusion."
Attribution: Brennan Manning. *Abba's Child: The Cry of the Heart for Intimate Belonging* by Brennan Manning, Ron Bennett, NavPress Publishing Group, 1994, 2002.

Chapter 11: "This, then, seems to be the work of the Spirit: to keep you vulnerable to live and love itself and to resist all that destroys the Life Flow."
Attribution: *Divine Dance* by Fr. Richard Rohr and Mike Morrell. Whitaker House, 2016.

All scripture quotes taken from the New King James Version® (NKJV®). HarperCollins Christian Publishing. www.harpercollinschristian.com. Originally commissioned by Thomas Nelson Publishers, 1975.